THE
BABY
BOAT

Also by Patty Dann

Mermaids

THE
BABY
BOAT

A Memoir of Adoption

PATTY DANN

HYPERION

NEW YORK

Library of Congress Cataloging-in-Publication Data
Dann, Patty.
    The baby boat : a memoir of adoption / Patty Dann. —
1st ed.
          p.   cm.
    ISBN 0-7868-6380-3
    1. Dann, Patty—Diaries. 2. Adoptive parents—United
States—Diaries. 3. Intercountry adoption—United States—
Case studies. 4. Intercountry adoption—Lithuania—Case stud-
ies. I. Title.
HV874.82.D3A3   1998
362.73'4'092—dc21
[B]   97-41748

Design by Jessica Shatan

FIRST EDITION

10   9   8   7   6   5   4   3   2   1

for Willem

THE
BABY
BOAT

I'd wanted a baby since I was eight years old. Sometimes it was tiny whispers behind my ears and sometimes it was a longing like a wound.

On our first date, my husband asked in his charming Dutch accent, "Do you want to get children?"

"Get children?" At first I did not understand, but quickly realized he meant "have a baby." I was then thirty-six years old and had never wed. I could feel the arsenal of eggs I'd been born with beginning to fray.

When I met my husband he had a Judaica calendar hanging in his kitchen, and I had a calendar of Amish quilts, which is of interest only because I am an American Jew and he is from Holland, the son of a Mennonite minister.

On our first date, Willem told me he was about to turn forty and had never wed.

We then had the discussion about "getting" children, and I politely explained that the proper expression was "having" a baby.

Growing up, my family did not go to temple, but on Sundays we often sat in the living room and read poetry and Bible stories and Emily Dickinson poetry. Some Sundays when my husband was young he played soccer or field hockey, but sometimes he traveled with his father the mornings he preached in neighboring towns. "Away games," his sisters called them. His father wore a black coat with tails when he preached.

"Life is a funny proposition," as my grandfather used to say. We were married by a female justice of the peace, at Staten Island Town Hall, with an old boyfriend of mine as my witness and an old girlfriend of Willem's as his. At ten o'clock in the morning we took the ferry from Manhattan. We got married at 11 o'clock, and then we went out for breakfast. Willem had eggs ranchero and I had a thumbstack of pancakes. That night, without our old lovers, we went to the circus.

❊   ❊   ❊

We knew, that first date, that we would wed. Both of us knew, but one of my students who had been married three times said, "You should know a man four seasons before you marry," and so we waited a year. At this time Willem was finishing up his doctoral dissertation on a seventeenth-century Dutch Reformed Church in Flatbush, Brooklyn. He had gone back for the degree while he worked as a historian at an international archive. I teach writing workshops because I'm addicted to stories. I often limit my classes to people who are at least fifty years old. "Eavesdrop" is the first word I remember learning, and I loved to sit at the grown-ups' table.

When I did not get "roundy," as the colonial women used to say, in our first year of marriage, my secret, personal belief from childhood was proven to be true: Babies don't come from making love. And then we "tried" to get pregnant, with the aid of calendars, thermometers, and charts, and still I was not in the family way. And then I got pregnant and felt more joyful than I ever had in my life. And then I had a miscarriage, and I wept and wept, and stood at the window watching the tugboats on the Hudson and whispered, "The baby boat. The baby boat was coming but it had to turn back."

And then and then and then the months rolled by.

"Don't try," people said. "Go on vacation." "Don't eat yogurt." "Don't think about it." "Stop running." "Stop swimming." "Do a handstand afterward."

I tried these things.

And then we went to a fertility doctor, a confident man with a waiting room with silk-and-brocade wallpaper, full of women whose longing for children filled the air with a cruel perfume.

Willem and I sat across from the doctor, with his big plastic replica of a woman's uterus, as he calmly explained, "We can inject you with hormones that come from nuns' urine that will build up your supply of eggs."

"Nuns' urine." I gasped.

"Yes, from a convent in Italy. It's very pure, no threat of disease."

I had entered another kingdom. And for a year Willem and I went through the maze of money and promises and needles in our quest to cradle a babe in our arms. We came up empty-handed and I felt like I was one hundred years old.

My friend Lydia sent me a fertility symbol from Brazil. Another friend gave me a cookie, made from a cabalistic cookie recipe that promised twins. Coleen, who adopted a baby from China, sent me a candle in the shape of the Venus of Willendorf. I don't want to talk about everything we did. It did not matter. I was not with child. I felt like a failure and I was angry I'd wasted so much money and possibly damaged my body with the fertility treatments. I was tired of working so hard at the most natural thing in the world. I felt out of the loop, but, in truth, I always have. On the most primitive level, I could never picture myself giving birth, but I always imagined being a mother.

"Are you going to throw me back?" I asked Willem.

"For a younger fish?" he asked. "I'm too tired," he said.

When I applied to college in 1970, there was a question on one of the applications. "What do you intend to be doing in twenty years?" I wrote that I wanted to have an orphanage and make books of photographs of the children. I frequently had dreams of walking into an orphanage and falling in love with a child.

The morning I turned forty, I awoke and whispered to Willem, "It's time to adopt."

"I think you'll get pregnant," he said, and I said nothing back.

I called a few of the adoption organizations listed in the yellow pages and asked for any written material. U.S. babies, South American babies, Asian babies, Eastern European babies. Brochures were spread out on the kitchen table like menus for take-out food. When I could coax Willem to talk about it, or at least have him listen to me talk about it, I said I wanted to adopt from overseas, from an orphanage.

One Saturday afternoon I announced I was going to a symposium on international adoption. I left the house clutching a notebook I'd saved from adolescence, full of furtive poems about phoenix rising. The hotel conference room was packed with wild-eyed people. This was the last stop on the road for many of us who'd spent our last savings on fertility treatments and now were looking at "the cost of one year of college tuition" just to start a family.

I immediately got a headache as the moderator

spoke about the three types of adoption: (1) agency initiated, (2) parent initiated, and (3) independent. "INDEPENDENT," I wrote down and underlined. I learned that basically means through a lawyer.

I lasted only forty-five minutes at the all-day affair. I've never been much of a comparative shopper. I just wanted a baby in the bathtub.

Willem wanted a baby as much as I did. We were never in disagreement about that, but he was still hoping I would give birth.

"Eastern Europe," I said to him one morning over breakfast.

"Eastern Europe?" he said.

"I think that's where our baby is. You're from Europe, my great-grandparents were from Europe. Maybe somehow there's a connection."

Willem observed my relentless research with a quiet restlessness fueled by hours of mutely watching baseball games on TV. I made so many phone calls my ears were sore. People told me we had to join a support group, to find out about the latest laws and requirements and for the camaraderie. I didn't want to. I wanted to be a mother. Adoption didn't scare me. Not being a mother did.

When I was a child I never knew anybody who was adopted. There was a rumor, never verified, about the kids of a family who moved away. And it was supposed to be a stage children went through, the fear that they were secretly adopted. After the stage ended they realized they were with their *real* parents after all.

That was my knowledge of adoption.

We heard of a female lawyer from a friend. "There's one catch," she said. "She's nocturnal. She works from seven at night till four in the morning, so she can make calls to Eastern Europe when it's early in the day their time. She'll drive you crazy in the long wait, but bottom line, you'll become parents, that's the bottom line."

I called and made an appointment to meet the lawyer several nights later.

Willem said, "We're just *talking* to this woman, right?"

"Right," I said, but I knew we'd begun the journey.

We drove in a hurricane last night, two hours to Connecticut, searching for the lawyer's office. We got lost and I begged Willem to stop and ask for directions, but he refused for thirty-five minutes. Our appointment was for 8 P.M. At eight thirty we were screaming at each other and I said if he didn't stop I'd open the door of the car. He finally pulled in at a seedy diner. I ran across the parking lot in the pouring rain, got garbled instructions, and on the way out of the restaurant, I fell in the wet parking lot and bloodied my elbow. We arrived forty-five minutes late.

The lawyer was a small, pretty woman who ushered us into her paper-stacked office immediately. She talked quickly, with a Polish accent, as she told us of her twelve years of adopting from all over Eastern Europe, how she had started as a divorce

11

lawyer and found this work much more satisfying. Right now she was having luck getting babies out of Lithuania. Willem and I sat across from her, both of us simmering with anger at each other. I tried to be as charming as I could be as she set out Christmas cards of babies and children whose adoptions she'd arranged on her desk. All the children were beautiful. I picked up the pictures and looked at them. I could love them. I glanced at Willem but could not read his face.

"Why were these children in orphanages?" I asked quietly. "Did their parents die?"

"Usually not," said the lawyer. "Sometimes they're single mothers, young women, sometimes they simply couldn't care for their children, but at birth they legally give up the rights to their babies. I'll give you a list of people I've gotten babies for. You can talk to them."

I always had an image of war orphans. Babies who desperately needed homes after their parents were killed fighting a worthy cause. This was different. I held the Christmas cards of these smiling children. What if the birth parents wanted them back?

Then the lawyer held out a list of everything we

had to do to adopt a child. I tried to cover the blood on my elbow and reached for the list.

REQUIREMENTS FOR ADOPTION

1. Birth Certificates from both spouses — originals, not copies.

Willem's birth certificate was in Utingeradeel, Holland, and I knew it would take awhile to track down. Mine was in New York and would be a bit easier.

2. Tax forms from previous two years.

We both got headaches showing people how much money we had or had not earned.

3. Letters from employers stating financial situation

We could do that. That meant everybody at work would know what we were doing. I didn't like people knowing everything about us.

4. Medical statements of health to prove fitness of parents

We'd have to have complete checkups. That wouldn't be a problem.

5. Statement from fertility specialist proving failed attempts to be parents

I hated the idea of having to go back to that doctor. I felt humiliated enough.

6. *Three detailed letters from friends to recommend us as parents*

What a strange thing. Nobody asked us to write recommendations for them when they became parents. They just had sex.

7. *Fingerprints for the FBI*

Great. We were possible criminals because we wanted a baby. I could feel myself turning red. I knew it was for the children, to protect the children. I tried to remain calm.

8. *Good conduct letters from the police department*

More evidence that we were not child molesters.

9. *The home study*

The lawyer explained that this was a three-hour intensive interview in our home, where a certified social worker would observe us and our environment. This was a crucial document and would take several months to write up.

10. *Forms for immigration and naturalization service*

I was dizzy. Willem looked furious.

"Thank you," we said.

"If you choose to work with me I ask for payment in three installments, one third when we start the procedure, one third when the baby is identi-

fied, and one third just before you travel to Lithuania."

On the frightening drive back through the pouring rain, Willem listened to a Yankees game and I
put my seat all the way back and shut my eyes,
sure we would crash, wanting to hold all those little
children on her desk. A fly ball was caught and
Willem pounded his fists on the steering wheel. I
felt profoundly alone and exhausted. I knew we
should talk to other lawyers as well, but I did not
have the strength. I reasoned that if she didn't do
her job well, she'd be out of work. But rational
thinking has not always been my forte; mainly I just
trusted her.

September 16, 1994

Last night we lay in bed wide awake at 3 A.M. and
I said quietly, "I have to be a mother, Willem, and
I don't see any other way."

"I'll try," he said. "What do I have to do?"

"Paperwork. We like paper, right? No needles,
no doctors. Sex when we want."

This morning I left a message on the lawyer's

answering machine saying we would like to work with her.

September 17, 1994

Today we went to have our fingerprints taken at the Twenty-fourth Precinct. The lobby was buzzing. There was a woman in handcuffs, a man in his underwear, and a battalion of cops in uniform. A woman with cat's-eye glasses and yellow Post-its stuck all over her sweater pointed up a stairway that said DANGER!! ASBESTOS!!! We climbed the stairs gingerly and entered a room full of overweight policemen sitting at desks. In the corner was the fingerprint station and a small jail cell, where a deranged man lay on the floor, cursing the day and all law enforcement officers. I clutched Willem's hand and we walked tentatively to the fingerprint desk. Nobody was there, and we waited as the man screamed, and we saw that the walls of the small cell were covered in angry fingerprints. Finally Officer Reilly appeared, a young man who put on plastic surgical gloves, then gently held each of our fingers and pressed them in the messy ink. I found it to be a sensual experience, him holding each of my fingers with those rubber gloves, and I felt far away from ever becoming a mother.

September 18, 1994

The lawyer called and said we also have to report every address we've lived at over the past twenty years to the New York State Government, so that they can do a computer check to see if we have any record of child abuse. All this child abuse talk keeps me from sleeping at night. Maybe I am a child abuser. What if the police checks find something? And every document has to be notarized. What curious people notaries are, but each time we get one of their stamps on our documents I caress the raised seal on the page and feel like I've been blessed by the Pope.

September 23, 1994

Tomorrow the social worker will come for the dreaded home study, to interrogate us to see if we will be fit parents, according to the all-American standards. In Connecticut you're not allowed to have a wood-burning stove in the house if you want to adopt, but this is not a problem in New York City. Willem's parents were divorced. My parents are divorced. We're old enough to be grandparents. We have leaks from the roof in our apartment, not a good environment for anybody. A painter came today to cover up some of the wet patches, a cosmetic job. I'm always skittish with workmen in the house, frightened I will fall in love with them and run away.

September 24, 1994 2 A.M.

I can't sleep. The social worker observed us today. I had made chocolate chip cookies to make it look like I'd be a wonderful mother, but she ate no cookies. She was a woman about our age, and she sat across from us for three hours, questioning us about ourselves, our marriage, our families, our past relationships.

"And what do you do if you have a disagreement?" she asked.

What we usually do is scream and scream and scream until we're both exhausted.

Willem said, "We like to go out for a walk and talk about it quietly."

I felt like we were on some kind of a talk show.

October 20, 1994

A single-space, ten-page report is complete, documenting more about us than most people would care to know. The report said we were a "friendly and focused couple who smile and laugh readily and appear to be compatible and eager to raise a family." We sound so lovely, I would like to be adopted by us.

December 1, 1994

We're home from a week in Amsterdam, where Willem defended his dissertation. Two of his friends stood by his side—*"paranimfen,"* they're called in Dutch, or "nymphomaniacs," as I call them—to mop his brow and give him water as he was interrogated. The Dutch professors, looking as if they were posing for a Rembrandt painting in their black robes and velvet hats, fired questions at him for precisely an hour. Then a man marched in carrying a scepter that he pounded on the ground. *"Hora est,"* he announced in Latin. "It is time," and the interrogation ceased immediately. At the party afterward, as Willem's family and friends talked loudly in Dutch, which sounded like wooden shoes knocking against my head, I sat, jet-lagged and tipsy, my thoughts spinning to the long nights when Willem sat at his computer deciphering church records written by candlelight in the seventeenth and eighteenth century. But mainly what was on my mind was that I now was on the same continent as my baby.

December 12, 1994

We have all the adoption paperwork done. The file bulges like a messy sandwich. Now the great wait begins. The paperwork is not difficult. In a strange way, checking off the items on the list makes us both feel we have some control over when and who will be our child, which, of course, is an illusion. When Willem tracked down his birth certificate from Utingeradeel we felt like we'd won the Grand Prix.

The lawyer says it will take three months for American immigration to clear everything and then three more months for Lithuania to do its dance. June. "Trust me, you wouldn't want to travel to Eastern Europe in winter, and it wouldn't be good to take the baby out then," she said.

December 23, 1994

"What are you going to raise your baby as?" people ask warily. "Are you going to convert it?" they demand, as if my child is a home appliance. The baby will probably be born of Catholic parents.

At a Christmas party, a Catholic friend confided that when her sister brought her adopted daughter home from the hospital, she stopped at Baskin-Robbins and baptized her in the drinking fountain. "It's good to baptize the baby, otherwise he'll end up in Limbo, and Limbo is not a good place to be."

21

"The mikvah," whispered a Jewish friend over the phone. "A ritual bath is good for the soul."

"As a Druid," I want to respond. I just want a peaceful home. I don't care what anybody calls God or whether they worship on Friday, Saturday, or Sunday. Maybe our child will end up a Hare Krishna.

Last night I saw on the news that it is snowing in Eastern Europe and I shivered, hoping my baby was warm, and later I woke up sobbing, sad for the mother who has to give up her child because she can't care for her or him. I woke up feeling cold for my baby and my baby's mother. In the adoption world I am the mother and the woman who gave birth is the birth mother, but at this point, 4,000 miles away, I'm nobody's mother yet.

January 1, 1995

A bitter cold day here. Last night, at midnight, we lit every candle we could find and made wishes for our baby. At some point this year, I believe we will go to Lithuania to pick up our child. Willem is more skeptical. He said I shouldn't get my hopes up, but I'm convinced we will. It's the only way I know how to get through this. The plan is to fly to Lithuania, stay the required week, then go back through Poland to the American Embassy. The baby will be an immigrant and therefore needs a green card. The Baltics — Estonia, Latvia, and Lithuania — don't issue immigration visas, only tourist visas, and I want my baby to be more than a tourist here. Every single person who hears we're adopting says "Do you have to go there and get the baby?" which surprises me. Going to get our baby will, I imagine, be the most exciting trip of our life.

February 22, 1995

Last night I dreamed we picked up our child, a three-month-old boy who could talk and walk. "I miss the wire," he said.

"What do you mean?" I said.

"The tightrope," he answered. "My family was in the circus."

"I'll see what I can do," I said.

February 23, 1995

I can't stop cleaning. I've cleaned out all the closets, all the drawers. I keep waiting for the phone to ring, even though I know I'll have to wait until spring, and I miss my father's mother, who died a few years go in Michigan. As each grandchild married a Christian she said, "And your people shall be of my people," and welcomed them. Her parents had come from Eastern Europe. She called the soap operas "the operas," and she loved watching football on television. Sometimes I wonder what my baby's grandparents did during the war. What did they think of Jews? But that will be my child's choice, if he wants to track down his roots. Being born five years after the war ended in Holland has left some kind of stain on Willem's soul. He's obsessed with whether people hid Jews or turned them in, what side they were on. I get a headache during these discussions. At this point I just want to smell the back of my baby's sweet neck.

March 14, 1995

My sister, who has three children and lives in Colorado, sent me a list of things I have to have for the baby, including baby scissors. "Cut the baby's nails at night when he's asleep," she wrote.

I also got a call from my friend Emily, an American married to a Dutchman who lives in Amsterdam. "Don't you know what Dutch women do?" she said. "They chew the baby's fingernails off."

March 17, 1995

I had an interview at a day care center, as a possibility for when I'm teaching, because I know the waiting list could take several years. There were two other women there, younger and more confident than I was, talking to each other about their children. When they turned and asked how old my baby was I was so embarrassed because I didn't know. When I told them I was adopting a child, I had a sensation of being physically ashamed, like I was a fraud.

We drove to Cooperstown this weekend to the Baseball Hall of Fame and James Fenimore Cooper's home. We have to get out of the house as much as possible or the phone will definitely not ring. I feel so close to Willem it frightens me, especially when we go on these little road trips. When we fight it is awful. I'm meaner than he is, at least in English, but sometimes he lets out a torrent of Dutch words, giving me a "taste of my own cookie dough," as they say in Dutch. But I don't understand exactly what he's saying. He wants to talk to our child in Dutch, and I'm scared that the two of them will talk behind my back. I love to teach Willem expressions he's never heard of, "the cat's pajamas," "top drawer." I love the way they sound in his Dutch mouth. But Dutch gets tangled in my throat, and I am ashamed I can't talk to my husband in his own language. Each time I visit his family they ask how my Dutch is, and I fumble a response. Not speaking a spouse's language is not an easy thing. Willem is convinced I'll finally learn Dutch as our child learns. We'll both be at the same level.

March 22, 1995

Now that I've told people we're adopting, and I blurt it out to everybody I meet, I'm exposed. Several people have suggested I should be more demure about it. I told everybody I was pregnant, and people warned me not to, to wait until it was a sure thing, but I did not. What I should do is join one of the adoption support groups, but I've never been able to sign up for anything.

April 18, 1995

It feels quite springlike to me, but there's no sign of a baby crawling down the road. I've tried not to call the lawyer, because she assured us she would call if there was any news. Advising us that we would be parents imminently is not a call she would overlook. But I broke down. As Willem fumed, I called her, and she checked on the baby's immigration papers. They still had not cleared with the INS. For two days I fell into a dark place, fearing I might never have a baby in my arms. But then the lawyer called back. Immigration had separated our fingerprints because I kept my maiden name, so my last name is of course different from Willem's. Our fingerprints from Willem's Dutch hands and my American hands and our baby's tiny Lithuanian hands are all separated. But the call from the lawyer cheered me. It was just a clerical error, and it was solved. We really will be a family. Twice I've been so surprised even to be married. The first time was returning to this country from a visit to Holland soon after we wed. The Customs form said, "Are you traveling with any other family members?" and at first I checked no. For so many years I had traveled alone, or with various beaux, certainly not any man to whom I was legally related. The second time was when I filled out the form for the day care center. PARENTS' OCCUPATIONS, it said, and I began to write down my own parents' jobs before I realized that they were talking about Willem and me.

May 29, 1995

It's Memorial Day, a rainy long weekend with Willem at home, and we cleaned the apartment again.

Willem pointed out that it is now the end of spring, and we don't have a baby. I said that adoption always takes longer than you think. Last week I developed a fear of being in the elevator when it is crowded, and twice I scurried out and walked up many flights of stairs.

May 31, 1995

I called the lawyer tonight. Several babies were born this month, she said, and hopefully one of those is our child. Mothers sign papers in the hospital when they cannot care for their babies, and then they're taken to the orphanages.

June 1, 1995

I went to the bookstore and bought a guide book to the Baltics. I've learned two words in Lithuanian. *"Laba diena,"* which means "Hello," is what I plan to say to the person who hands me my child; then I'll say *"Laba diena"* to my baby. And I learned *"Aciu,"* which sounds like a sneeze, "achoo," and means "thank you." That's what I plan to say after I'm handed my baby.

June 10, 1995

We have heard no news. The lawyer says we have to wait. The laws are changing every few weeks in Lithuania, which has been a democracy only since 1991. The country is in the midst of enormous changes. After each time I talk to the lawyer, Willem gets angry, and then I get angry at him for getting angry at her. "Maybe we should think of it like racing cars," I said. "When cars are speeding around a track and there's a disabled car in the middle of the course, the drivers try to steer toward the wreck, because they're not in that much control. It's the one place they won't hit." (This was something a boyfriend told me years ago.) "It's the same with the lawyer," I said. "We should realize things will never ever go according to plan in this process. And then we won't be disappointed. We will not get the call when we expect it and we won't have our baby when we've been told we will."

Willem doesn't say I'm crazy out loud. He just shakes his head and fumes.

We went to dinner with our friends Piet and Kathleen. He is Dutch and she is American and they want a baby as well. Before dinner the men talked in Dutch, about what I can't be sure, while Kathleen and I spoke in English about our longing for babies. She is a therapist who works with babies born addicted to drugs and also with abused infants. I told her I was afraid someone might hurt my baby in the orphanage, and she said the saddest cases were not those who were hit but the babies who were not held, and I prayed that someone was rocking my baby gently. At dinner we all spoke English. Piet said his father had originally studied for the priesthood, and the last class of the day for the boys was smoking class. Each boy took out a small wooden box of matches and tobacco and cigarette papers and learned to roll their cigarettes and all the etiquette of lighting and puffing. "Because," said Piet, "it was very important in the small Dutch villages for the priests to smoke, both cigars and cigarettes." In the end, Piet's father became a pediatrician. Piet's mother is one of the remarkable women in Holland who visits people's homes after babies are born to teach new mothers how to care for the infants and serve tea to guests. I wondered if the men had married Dutch women and we had married Americans, would we all have babies by now.

June 12, 1995

Willem and I ran a ten-kilometer race on Shelter Island, a small island between the North Fork and the South Fork of Long Island. It was a glorious day, with a good sunny breeze, and I felt strong enough to be a mother at forty-one. As the gun went off I shut my eyes for a second and felt the seventeenth-century women colonists who settled the island running beside me in their long dresses, their long curls falling out of their hairpins.

June 14, 1995

Last night we put together the crib. I put in a small doll I had made thirty-five years ago in a sewing class and a tiny teddy bear I got for my sixth birthday. On that birthday it was Daylight Savings and my parents turned the clocks the wrong way by mistake. They turned the clocks one hour forward instead of back, and my friends were two hours late. I cried and the tears stained my dress.

I stood looking at the crib for a long time and then I kissed the doll and the bear good night.

July 3, 1995 11 P.M.

The lawyer just called and said that we have a baby girl! She said she'll have more details in a week. She thinks we'll travel in August. She also said that some of the judges were on vacation and that they were renovating the hospital where our daughter was born. Willem and I hugged each other, but we both said at the same time "The racing car theory," and we tried to contain our excitement. Renovating the hospital, what exactly does that mean?

July 6, 1995

Last night we woke up at 3 A.M. We were so excited we couldn't sleep, so I made scrambled eggs and toast. We sat in the dark kitchen, quietly eating, wide awake, full of the notion that we are parents to a baby girl in Lithuania. We named her last night, but I'm frightened to say it aloud or even write it down until we know when we'll travel to pick her up.

July 11, 1995

I bought my daughter a tiny dress, dotted with rose petals, to wear in court. Will she want to wear a dress? Will it feel strange after her hospital and orphanage clothes? I hemmed it last night, because it looks so long, but I have no idea what size she is.

July 12, 1995

I bought eight rolls of paper towels, eleven sponges, and six bottles of lemon-lime soda. I keep stocking up, feeling like a supply of household goods will prepare me for motherhood. I've been nesting for ten months now.

Over and over again, people ask us the same questions:

1. *Will you know the medical history of the baby?*
We'll know a bit—the child's health since birth—but nothing more, such as what other relatives died of.
2. *Will a doctor examine the baby?*
Yes, in Lithuania, and then again in Poland by a doctor approved by the American government, because the child will be an immigrant. Just like an adult who is applying for a green card is examined.
3. *What will you know about the birth mother?*
This question always throws me, and is asked the most frequently. I will know that she was wise enough and loved her baby enough to know she couldn't care for the child, but I won't know all the intricate secrets of her genes.

4. *What will you know about the birth father?*
Probably even less.

5. *Why does it take so long?*
A fair question, but I don't think Americans would be so eager to send their children to far-off lands. Bureaucracy, red tape, constantly changing laws. Nothing particularly rational.

6. *Can you choose the sex of the child?*
You can, but there are no guarantees.

7. *Will you get a photograph?*
Perhaps, but I'm ready to love a child, whatever he or she looks like.

Deep in my soul, I don't understand why people want to know the answers to these questions. If I were pregnant I would have little idea what my baby would look like, what bundle of genes he or she would have. I could take every test in the world but I would not know the health of the baby until birth. I'm beginning to become a mother already, so these questions fall on my ears like an assault, as if people are questioning our judgment or, even worse, trying to figure out if my child will be a healthy and upstanding citizen. Just who are we letting into the neighborhood? I'm beginning to sense that as open-minded as many people are, there's still a prejudice toward adopted children. Maybe it's like white people's prejudice toward blacks. They love them when they're cute little babies, but when they grow up, they're on guard. I have a friend, D., who is fifty, who was adopted a few days after he was born but doesn't like people to know. He says he's secretive because often when he's told people, that becomes his main identity, an ADOPTED PERSON, and he's not pleased with all the images that are associated with the label.

July 14, 1995 Bastille Day

It is 98 degrees today. Watching the news about the war in Bosnia makes me numb. I saw some footage from an orphanage where a little boy was, and probably is still, knitting endlessly, his only link with his dead mother. It is over 100 degrees in Eastern Europe. I picture my baby sweaty in a crib and I want to be the one to soothe her with a damp cloth, on the back of her neck, behind her knees, to lick the tears from her crying eyes. I already feel fierce as a wolf in my desire to protect her.

July 17, 1995

Twice people said to me today, "I know you'll get pregnant as soon as you adopt." But I'm not thinking about a second child at this point. When people are pregnant, nobody says "I know you'll get pregnant again." According to my personal poll, 85 percent of what people say is said from a good heart, to comfort, but it often ricochets in my ears like a harsh tambourine.

July 18, 1995

I spoke on the phone to a woman today who has adopted two babies. I get so many phone calls from people I've never met, I feel like I'm on the Underground Railroad. This woman was very firm with me. "Don't think you're saving anybody," she said. "You're adopting because you want a family. Adoption is the most selfish thing in the world. You'll hear people say over and over 'Oh, the baby's so lucky,' but, sweetheart, you're the lucky one."

Saving the world, I confess, is something that has

crossed my mind several times in my life. When I was sixteen, in 1968, I wanted to save the world, and I went to Oklahoma to live with the Ponca Indians. I worked in a day care center in the awful heat, under the catalpa trees, and I made many mistakes. But the Indian girls welcomed the Jewish girl from New York. They braided my hair, made me a turquoise shawl, taught me how to dance and eat delicious, greasy squaw bread. They ended up adopting me.

July 20, 1995

The lawyer called last night. I answered the phone, as usual, mainly because Willem shows no acknowledgment of a ringing phone. I think this is an initiation into the world of mothers: one woman talking to another about a child. There has been another delay, the lawyer said. The law has changed in Lithuania. The new law states that babies cannot be legally adopted until they're at least three months old.

The birth mothers have the right to take back the babies in this time period, as do the birth fathers and even the grandparents, but they rarely do, the lawyer said. She *thinks* we will travel in the fall.

"What month?" I said, "What month in the fall?"

"September or October," she said.

I felt strangely calm. I like fall. Autumn is good. After all, we knew delays are the name of the game. "But do we still have the same baby girl?" I asked evenly.

At this point Willem looked up from the paper with a stunned expression.

"Yes," she said, "I'm going over there next week and I'll see her."

"Oh," I said. "Okay." See her, see my child, before I see my child.

"Okay," I repeated. "Well, thank you, okay, okay, thank you very much."

And I hung up.

I did not want to look at Willem.

"Okay, there's been a delay," I said, with my back to him, facing the refrigerator.

"She's crazy," he said.

"No, she's going to get us a baby. Please don't start this. I know we're going to get a baby. I'm going to bed."

I lay in bed, alone, naked, sweating, with the fan pointed at my feet. I felt very far from Willem. I need his support. We have to stay optimistic about this or we won't get through it. I don't have the energy to convince him we'll have a baby. I should join one of those damn support groups.

July 21, 1995

I notice people looking at my breasts when they talk to me, not like when I was eighteen and had big, firm breasts and I was horribly embarrassed, but now it's a fleeting glance. Women do it as well as men, as if they're thinking "She looks like she can get pregnant. I wonder what's wrong."

July 22, 1995

I went to the shoe store to buy sandals. I have the whole summer to walk through without a baby. I felt compelled to tell the man kneeling at my feet that we were adopting a baby from Lithuania.

"Lithuania? Do the Russians own that? There's a guy from the Chicago Bulls from there."

"That's Croatia," I say. Willem has filled me in on each of the Eastern European basketball players in the NBA.

"Yeah," says the shoe salesman, "Something like that."

I bumped into one of my neighbors in the shoe store, an elderly gentleman who introduces himself as "the maestro."

"Ah, Lithuania," he said. "They have the most beautiful dancers, the most beautiful legs, and Baryshnikov was born in Latvia."

July 23, 1995

Last night I woke up gasping from a nightmare where I saw a row of babies tossing and turning and our adoption file was scattered all over the floor. I couldn't find my birth certificate and I kept searching and searching for it endlessly.

July 24, 1995

I've been reading the guidebook on Lithuania. Lithuanian is one of the oldest surviving languages in the world and it's related to Sanskrit. There are thirty-two letters. Our daughter has heard all these letters by now in her few weeks on earth. I wonder if there's a word for birth mother in Lithuanian. It's such an awkward term, like some kind of caveman talk—birth mother, birth mother, birth mother. And I keep thinking of this woman, is she missing her daughter, her birth daughter? Is she crying?

July 25, 1995

I am missing my father's mother again. Dorothy met my grandfather, Moe, in Canton, Ohio, at a small gathering in someone's home. Six months later he sent her a New Year's card. And then he visited. "When he came to call," she said, "it was raining, and he offered to share his umbrella with me. Now, I *had* my own umbrella," said Dorothy, "but with Moe I knew that was a proposal."

Dorothy and Moe begat my father and his brother and sister.

I am also missing my mother's mother, even though she is alive and well and lives nearby. My grandmother, Vivian, went to work at my grandfather Sam's business, a paper company, when she was nineteen years old. "I chose paper because paper is clean," he said. "Paper is a good, clean business." When he interviewed Vivian he asked, "If you write down numbers in a book, would you write on both sides of the page?"

"Oh, no," she answered, she who had received the top science award in high school, "I always leave one side blank in case I have to add new orders." And so she was hired as the bookkeeper. After a few weeks she told the girls in the office she would be going to Atlantic City for the weekend, and Sam overheard. He went all the way down to meet her on the train, but she wasn't there. She hadn't felt well, apparently, and canceled the trip at the last minute. The next week, back at the office he teased, "That wasn't a very nice thing to do," and soon after they were married.

Vivian and Sam begat my mother and her sister.

My parents met in an elevator at Rockefeller Center where they were both working for NBC radio. My mother says my father was waving his hands around pretending to be an orchestra conductor. My father gave my mother a pair of sneakers because she ran around the office so much. My parents begat my brother, sister, and myself.

And my baby, my daughter? Who begat her? Did her father love her mother? Had they courted for a long time? Did they meet at the office or in the fields? Was she wearing perfume? Did he smell of sweat or aftershave? Was there American music playing on the radio? Who begat my child?

Some days I have the sense that when I finally have my baby, her arrival will be my birth. She will beget me.

July 26, 1995

I keep updating assignments for my students. They don't have to do them, but I have a list of over two hundred memories now. Some students say they have so many memories the assignments make them focus. Others say they have forgotten so much it helps them remember. The list is simple, but the students write remarkable things.

New shoes, baseball, roller skating, telephone, rain, joy during war, a crush, laundry, haircut, tea or coffee, grandparent, aunt, uncle, a bicycle . . . I wish I could ask the birth parents of my child to write about these things. At the same time, it's easier for them to remain anonymous in my mind. Some people have said to me they couldn't handle knowing so little about the birth parents, but I see that as my daughter's choice for when she's older.

July 27, 1995

Today in my mailbox at work, I received a large envelope written in a formal hand with a beautiful Swiss stamp of a peacock. It was from my student, Ernst, a gentleman near eighty. "Pink or blue?" he wrote. "I want to bring your baby a gift from Switzerland. Please write me at the following address," and he gave me his address at Lake Geneva. Ernst fled Germany as a refugee with his young wife. Now he is a widower, back vacationing in Europe.

All these older people are so kind to me, and I'm frightened one of them will die. I wrote to Ernst that we *think* we'll have a baby girl. What I wanted to do was write and ask if he would go sneak a look at her, but I restrained myself.

July 28, 1995

Yesterday one of Willem's sisters called, a rare event. Mennonites, unlike Jews, don't seem to be people of the phone. He has three sisters, and they're all younger. The youngest of the three called. She is in charge of a Dutch organization that commemorates the end of World War II every year. And this year she was interviewed on television and a Jewish woman contacted her. It seems that Willem's grandparents, his mother's parents, had hidden her during the war. Would Willem have hidden me? He says he would like to think so. But would I have hidden someone if I were in that position? It's hard to say. I barely like having people over for dinner.

Willem's mother's father was a stock broker, and he and his wife had three daughters. Willem's father's father was a math teacher and his wife was active in the Mennonite Church and traveled all over the world. They were from the town of Zwolle. They had four children. Three survived.

July 29, 1995

Today we received a letter from our foster child in India.

Dear Foster Parents:
Good morning. As your foster child is unable to write, the village animator writes this letter. Here the summer goes on. There is no rainfall and the cattles feel sad. Summer increases hot. We send loving to you and your family circle. Rest in the next.

I feel the same way. I just wish my family circle was a little larger. Most of my friends are having trouble getting pregnant. I know one family with five daughters, and the mother always said she got pregnant whenever she made French toast for her husband, but so far she has only one grandchild. Maybe it's the end of evolution. There's a rumor going around that there's a woman who gave birth naturally in the neighborhood, but nobody has actually met the woman.

July 30, 1995

Today we got a letter from friends in Holland who are desperate to have a child, but in liberal Holland, where you're allowed to be a prostitute and shoot up heroin and God knows what, you're not allowed to adopt a baby if you're over forty years old. In fact, it's more precisely peculiar — the combined number of years you and your mate are over forty is the age of the child you're entitled to. Hence, Willem and I could adopt a six-year-old . . . We have, half jokingly, said we would get two babies in Lithuania and give one to our friends. Of course that is highly illegal. At the rate we're going, maybe we'll end up adopting an older child. Maybe our daughter will just come over here, get off the plane, and go straight to college.

July 31, 1995

It is a hot, oppressive day in New York. I want to run away, live alone in a cottage somewhere where I can go to bed early, get up before dawn, sweep the floors, and write. I want to run away from my husband and my students. Or could I run away to Paris like I did when I was twenty-one and ate pain au chocolate twice a day and took karate classes four times a week at the Centre Franco-Vietnamien. I also worked as a baby-sitter there, for a two-year-old boy. He was always hungry and I was always hungry. My pockets that year were sticky with custard and chocolate.

Late at night of July 31. I don't know what time . . .

We are surprised we're having a daughter. People have told us that mostly boys are adopted from Eastern Europe. We're having a daughter or we have a daughter. I don't know which to say. Willem grew up with girls, but he longed for a brother. He even had imaginary brothers. He named them all and they raced their bicycles to school with him along the canals and of course they trained for the Tour de France together. I have a brother who lives on the West Coast and we talk only once in a blue moon, but I do have a picture of him kissing me when he was four and I was three.

August 1, 1995

It is my mother's mother's ninety-first birthday. She says she is waiting for our baby. I've always preferred the company of older people. Her name is Vivian, but on her birth certificate it only says Female. Her parents called her Rivi, but when she got to school her teacher said, "There is no such name as Rivi. We will call you Rebecca." And that is the name on her high school diploma. When she graduated she changed her name to Vivian. She just told me this today.

August 2, 1995

Yesterday I asked my students to write about their names for fifteen minutes in class. One man's mother, who had desperately wanted a girl, dressed him in frills and named him Frank but called him Franny. One woman wrote of fleeing Germany and landing in America in 1943. The first thing she did was choose a new name from a phone book she found in a telephone booth. When I was ten I tried to make people call me "Mango."

Three months ago, one spring weekend, I hand-made baby announcements, one hundred cards and envelopes. The announcements say WITH GREAT JOY WE WELCOME . . . and when we finally get word to fly over for our baby I'll fill in her name and birth date. Willem said, "Why don't you write invitations to her sixteenth birthday party while you're at it?"

August 3, 1995

There were men working in the locker room at the pool where I swim. Whenever women were in the showers the men put towels over their heads so they wouldn't see us. Standing naked in front of a construction worker with a towel thrown over his head made me feel sexier than I had in years.

This afternoon we got a package in the mail from Utrecht, Holland, from Willem's oldest sister (a year younger than he is). She is six feet tall and makes me feel I should brush my hair, but she's extremely generous and punctual about sending gifts. Now she has sent a tiny beige-and-white dress sewn by Willem's mother, whom I never met. There was also a little red doll called a theosophist doll. I'm not sure what that means, but I put her in the crib alongside the doll I made.

August 4, 1995

I found Willem wide awake and reading at four thirty this morning. He looked up from his newspaper and said, "What exactly is the lawyer doing? What does she do all day?"

"I don't know. She's in Lithuania now. I'll call one of the people she's adopted for. They'll know. Laura says we'll end up with a baby who wants to get out of bed all the time and you'll wish you could stay in bed longer. She says that's the main difference between children and grown-ups all over the world."

"Well, fine for Laura," said Willem. "But I need to know what's going on."

August 5, 1995

Today I called one of the women who had adopted two children through our lawyer. The kids were giggling and pressing on the phone buttons, so it was a fragmented conversation, and we did get disconnected after about five minutes, but I was able to glean the following information:

1. The lawyer has between fifty and one hundred clients at a time, so there is some kind of waiting list *2.* She travels to a variety of Eastern European countries, depending on the most recent adoption laws. And the laws change constantly, with no warning. There are elections of special adoption committees and pressure groups opposed to foreign adoption. When the laws change, all the paperwork that has been filed under the old laws must be redone, and they're not talking state-of-the-art electronic communications systems here. It's a lot of talking and waiting and waiting and stacks of paper, and papers getting misplaced. *3.* There are people in Eastern Europe who want to adopt as well, and they have priority. *4.* This lawyer finds healthy babies. Sometimes babies are healthy at birth and then get sick. Sometimes very sick . . . *5.* "But mainly," this woman said, "she doesn't want to tell you too much until you're ready to fly. I know you're going crazy, but — " and then her kids disconnected the phone again.

August 6, 1995

I can't stop thinking of my baby's feet. I wonder if they're swaddled in Lithuanian slippers. I even gave my students the assignment to write about a memory of shoes. They wrote about high-button shoes and spats and spikes. When Willem was a child his mother had the four children march barefoot around the table on a rough mat every night to toughen their feet.

For my fortieth birthday, Willem and I went to Toronto for the weekend. I had just had a miscarriage and when we wandered around the Bata Shoe Museum and came to a tiny pair of baby slippers, I had to look away.

August 7, 1995

This heat is making me batty. I would like to be in Friesland, the farmland in the north of Holland where we stayed in Willem's aunt and uncle's cottage three years ago. Every morning we rose early and wrote on two different sides of a ping-pong table, then had lunch of strong cheese and fresh bread from the local bakery. Each afternoon we cycled through the fields and past the lakes that were full of boats with plum-colored sails. Every evening after dinner, while the sun blazed until ten P.M. we dragged the ping-pong table outside and played five games. Then we ate fresh strawberries and whipped cream from the farmer's cows next door and Willem told me stories about the village nearby, where he was born in a parish house on his parents' bed.

3 A.M.

I can't sleep. I am reading the book *What to Expect the First Year.* At two months a baby should be able to smile in response to your smile. The baby might be able to roll over and say "ah-goo" or a similar vowel-consonant.

I pace the living room. Is my baby smiling at someone else's smile? Is someone else smiling at my baby? It is seven hours later there, so it is morning in Lithuania. Is my baby able to say "ah-goo," or do Lithuanian babies make other baby sounds?

August 9, 1995

My students wrote about crying. I read an article recently that insisted men cried more in the Middle Ages. You could see men weeping, knights rusting in their armor outside the castle walls, or shepherds burying their faces in piles of wool. I have never cried much. People keep telling me how sad I must be. But that really is not the main emotion. I was sad I could not bear a child, but now I am awaiting my child. I've had students write about how after they survived cancer their lives seemed so much richer but that some people didn't understand, still wanted to pity them. Perhaps that's what I feel. Now that I've begun this adventure, as difficult as it is, my life is bigger.

August 10, 1995

There are 3.5 million people in Lithuania. In 1385 eleven-year-old Princess Jadviga of Poland was betrothed to Wilhelm von Hapsburg. The wedding was supposed to take place in Cracow, which was then capital of Poland. But in the midst of the wedding celebrations, with dancing and merriment going on, a delegation of Lithuanian nobles conferred with the Poles and made a new plan. Little Jadviga would not marry a Hapsburg. She was now betrothed to the Lithuanian grand prince, who was three times her age and had murdered many of her relatives. This was not a happy marriage, and Jadviga died, childless, at twenty-four.

August 13, 1995

Yesterday, while I was sorting through my letters at the mailbox at the YMCA, a fellow teacher came up to me, a poet, and said, "I used to know how to say 'Is the wind in your face?' in Lithuanian," and I felt a rush through my body, with the thought that someday my daughter would learn the words "wind" and "face," and that I might be with her when she does, and I hoped a nurse was holding her and gently blowing on her eyelids to cool her off.

August 14, 1995

Einstein said "I want to know God's thoughts. The rest are details," but I woke up with this list in my head:

1. Get formula fortified with iron, Pampers, baby clothes *2.* Read student work *3.* Wash windows in baby's room *4.* Write two chapters in new novel *5.* Get baby

August 15, 1995

Willem is edgy but quiet. Last night at 3 A.M. he woke up, and whenever he wakes up I wake up, even when he's silent. I whispered that when our little baby comes I promise not to send him away. Each time his mother gave birth to his three sisters he was sent away to stay at his grandparents. Willem patted me on the arm. I turned on the light and we found a ladybug on my pillow. He said, "In Dutch they're called 'Our Dear Lord Beast.' They're good luck. You count their age by the number of dots on their back."

August 16, 1995

The lawyer called and said, "Are you sure you don't want a family unit?"

"What's that?" I asked cautiously.

"More than one child? Siblings?"

Willem was reading the paper on the couch. "Hold on," I said.

I put my hand over the receiver. "Do we want more than one child?" I hissed at him.

Willem looked dazed.

I got back on the phone. "I think one at a time," I said. "Thank you for calling."

Today I had lunch with my friend Karen. At birth she was given away by her mother to her childless aunt, because her mother already had so many children. Karen said the tragedy came when her mother wanted her back and Karen was forced to leave her aunt at eight years old. She said the second time she was given up felt like the adoption.

August 17, 1995

Last night I could not sleep and tiptoed out of the bedroom. I dragged the big atlas off the shelf and lay on the living room floor and turned to the Baltics. I traced my finger around the outline of Lithuania, shut my eyes, and imagined tracing the outline of my daughter's face. Even the most intelligent people ask me "Where exactly is Lithuania?" and I say "Northeast of Poland," as if I've been there. But I had to look it up. Until I knew my child was there I had no idea that Latvia, Estonia, and Lithuania combined are the size of the state of Washington. I stared at the Gulf of Finland, Riga Bay, and the Baltic Sea. I want to swim in that gulf, in that bay, and in that sea.

August 20, 1995

Today an old boyfriend called, one of the men I tried so hard *not* to get pregnant with. From the time my mother slipped me a light blue book, the exact color of the Kotex box, called *It's Time You Knew*, all about the birds and the bees, my goal was to not get pregnant. All I remember from the book was that it said that boys can be wolves in the back of cars. They simply *cannot* control themselves. I frankly wouldn't mind being with a wolf-boy in the back of a car on this end-of-summer day, some- where out in the woods, perhaps in Oregon.

I spent three years at the University of Oregon af- ter I drove across the country with three friends. We were all fleeing colleges in the East. We would each drive a tank of gas and then switch off, day and night, night and day. This was before the 55 mph speed limit, and we got there at dusk after four days and pulled off our clothes and jumped in the Willamette River. Then we stole corn from a field and cooked it over a fire. Yes, I would like to be doing that now, rather than waiting for the plumber to come.

August 21, 1995

One of my students died. As a friend so subtly pointed out, "You're not teaching kindergarten." I understand that, but it takes my breath away each time.

August 25, 1995

Yesterday I was doing exercises at the reservoir in Central Park when I noticed two men next to me, stretching their legs. One man, quite attractive, with a deep tan, was wearing sunglasses and staring at me as I swiveled my hips. Well, I thought, it's been a long time since anybody's looked at me like that. I began my run around the reservoir with a new bounce to my step. Three quarters of the way around I heard two men talking behind me. "You can do it, watch out, there's someone in front of you. You've almost done it," and I realized the man was blind. I turned briefly and saw it was my suitor in sunglasses.

August 30, 1995

The lawyer called. There will be another delay. Paperwork is held up in Lithuania. It will be October before we can get our daughter. I will be forty-two in October. I am weary. I called my grandmother, not to tell her, just to hear the sound of her voice. For over forty years I've known her number by the prefix GR-3, never just the numbers. I dialed it now for the great comfort of hearing her answer her rotary phone.

September 4, 1995

We went to a Labor Day picnic on a lake, "in the country," as city people say.

At one point a woman I barely know pulled me by the elbow and muttered, "See that woman there sitting alone under the umbrella? Don't look now," which of course made me twist my head around to stare.

There was, in fact, a perfectly normal-looking woman reading in the shade.

"Well," my confidante continued, "she adopted a child, and then eighteen years later gave birth to a daughter! So, you never know what will happen to you."

In eighteen years I'll be sixty, but I tried to give her an earnest look of thanks.

When we returned from the picnic, there was a sheet of paper under our door along with two menus from Chinese restaurants. I figured it was a notice about the water being turned off in the building or a block party, and was about to stuff it in the garbage when I saw the words "Adoption Support Groups." I stood in the kitchen reading the list of a half-dozen groups, from RESOLVE, the national organization, to all the local churches and synagogues. "Come get information," the notice said, "legal counseling and emotional support at our monthly meetings."

September 7, 1995

Last night when I could not sleep I did not decide to call any support groups. Instead I rustled through boxes in the closet and discovered a stack of my childhood diaries. They are brown leather with gold designs on the covers and some even have gold-trimmed pages for my important entries. There are locks, and the keys went astray long ago, but I found they opened quite easily with a bobby pin. The first I opened was from 1963. I was ten years old. I had carefully put my weight at 54 pounds and my height at 48" on the first page.

On November 22, 1963, my entry was as follows:

GRIEF & SORROW

On this tragic day, our one leader who protected and cared for us, who all but those who wished to disgrace our nation, looked up to, was killed. How disgraceful it is. Let all men be ashamed of themselves and speak out. Let that man sacrifice himself through torture or anything else as is fitting and proper. Our President was shot by the disgraceful. All day there was no entertainment, no music, only praying and what was fitting. We not only prayed for our President John F. Kennedy but for our country that is in disgrace. This may not be very poetic but it's the only way I can describe the tragic, tragic happening to our beloved President John F. Kennedy. Amen. Thank you.

There are benefits to adoption. My child will not be burdened with my peculiar genes.

Entry from June 11, 1966:

I am very sorry my handwriting is so messy. My mother tells me to relax, but I cannot relax when I write. Please God, do you think I'm a good person?

September 8, 1995

Kathleen came over for lunch and we tried not to, but all we could talk about was her wanting a baby and me waiting for a baby. We finally got off the subject and she noticed the small photograph of a mother elephant and her baby stuck inside the refrigerator on one of the side walls. I put it there the day I moved into my apartment twelve years ago, with plans to decorate the whole inside, but the elephants were as far as I got. During lunch Kathleen confided that she had recently paid for a woman to come to their apartment, a "feng shui" specialist, she is called, who helps arrange your furniture to create the best energy in your home. This feng shui lady told Kathleen and Piet to leave the dust under their bed if they really wanted to have a baby. Maybe that's been my problem all along. Maybe I should never have spent all those years reaching under the bed with the long handle of the vacuum.

When Kathleen left I had the sudden urge to buy Willem a pair of shoes. He never buys shoes for himself, and I figured that when I had my daughter I'd have no time to help him shop. So I hurried to the shoe store a few blocks down the street. The store was full of schoolkids jumping around, and I felt dizzy. I've never liked groups of children, not as a child and not now as a grown-up, and I felt scared to have a baby. I did manage to buy a pair of sneakers for Willem and hurried back home with the box. I've always felt guilty shopping and tend to throw away all evidence — box, bags, any wrapping in garbage cans on the street — and stuff the items into my bag. I controlled myself and kept the box, though, aware that I might have gotten the wrong size. I sat clutching the box of shoes, watching the news and waiting for Willem to get home from work. Packwood has just been forced out of the Senate "for kissing," as he said. The O. J. trial is dragging on and on and on. The young woman who tried to enter the Citadel Military Academy was all dolled up on Oprah, followed by the sixteen-year-old who had sex with the Rhodes Scholar Ohio congressman. I held the box of shoes tight. The thought of raising a daughter in this country petrifies me.

September 13, 1995

Last night on the news there was a piece on young women in England who had moved into tree houses to voice their objection to razing the forest to build a superhighway. It was the most extraordinary scene, these strong young women hoisting themselves into their homes in the branches. I wonder if my daughter will live in a tree house some day. One thing my daughter will definitely not do is wear the tiny flowered summer dress I bought her to wear in court. The weather is turning cool now, and by the time we get to Lithuania there might even be a frost. The little dress sits patiently in the closet, and next summer it will be too small for my daughter.

September 15, 1995

Last night Willem and I did not like each other. We bristled around the apartment like porcupines. At one point I lay down on the couch with the lights out. Strands of clarinet music came from the rooftop next door. A lone clarinetist was playing "America the Beautiful," a song I had not heard in years. When it came to "From sea to shining sea" I burst into tears, for the loss of my childhood and the loss of the dream of bearing a child.

September 18, 1995

We got up at five on Saturday morning to drive to Albany for an all-day, all-evening affair for colonial Dutch scholars. People gave talks for hours on colonial Dutch people as if they were still alive. I had to fight to stay awake, but I rallied when I heard a woman talk about pirates who kept stacks of flags on deck and flew different colors to pretend they were from different countries, and when another scholar tried to prove that a certain shipwreck must have occurred on a moonless night. We were also invited to a colonial dinner. A woman had called and said to me, "It is not black tie, and please, no off-the-shoulder dresses." I found this curious. Did it have something to do with the prudery of the colonial Dutch? Had some risqué rumor preceded me in particular? The only time I wore anything off the shoulder was as a little girl, when I wore my nightgown pulled down low to impress a boy baby-sitter. At the colonial meal I wore a dress that covered my shoulders and everything else and had so much wine and port and game birds and stuffing and chocolates and meringues that I had a strong out-of-century desire to loosen my corset.

After the conference we visited friends of Willem who live in an eighteenth-century farmhouse with lots of dogs. Amid stacks of books and shards of crockery from colonial life, the husband immediately sat down at his computer and found pages and pages on the Internet about adoption. When I hear the term "Web site" two things always come to mind—"Charlotte's" and "Eensy Weensy Spider." I use my own computer like a typewriter and will leave it to my child to teach me the world of on-line. But if I do ever get the courage to learn, the screen is full of meticulous data on International Adoption—all the agencies, as well as country-by-country information issued from the State Department.

I immediately learned that last year 9,679 children were adopted internationally and immigrated to the United States; ninety-five were from Lithuania.

The one page I did ask our host to print out was a list of Famous Adopted People from the National Adoption Clearing House.

I was delighted to see such a varied list, from John J. Audubon (naturalist), to Dave Thomas (founder of Wendy's). But it warmed my heart to see Marilyn Monroe (actress) nestled in the list with Moses (biblical leader).

October 4, 1995

Yesterday O. J. Simpson was set free and I burst into tears. On the street people were cheering. And now the Pope is coming. It's too much for me to bear and my daughter is missing it all.

October 5, 1995

Today I took the train to Washington, D.C., to visit my mother, and we went to a collection of rare French manuscripts at the Library of Congress. I've gone on outings like this with her since I was a baby. I stared long and hard at the illuminated pages of Christine de Pisan, 1364 to "some time after 1429" it said in the catalog, who was supposedly the first female writer to earn her living from a pen. One day when I was a child I became convinced that I was destined to make illuminated manuscripts and my dear mother tracked down some gold ink and as close to parchment paper as she could get, and I set to work. I hope I will be as devoted a mother.

My train back to New York was stuck, on the

track at Menlo Park, New Jersey, in the midst of Hurricane Opal, for four hours. When I finally got home I found Willem setting up pots and bowls under leaks that were streaming through the ceiling.

October 6, 1995

The hurricane has passed, and I awoke to sunshine and full pails of water around the bed. I decided to run around the reservoir to clear my head, and as I did, I heard rock music blaring from loudspeakers and the chant "John Paul II, We love you!" They were the performers preparing for tomorrow's 7 A.M. concert before the Pope's mass. I felt a gleeful calm and ran much faster than usual.

October 12, 1995

I slept fitfully. I always do at the beginning of a semester, scared the students will discover I'm an impostor.

October 13, 1995

The lawyer called from Eastern Europe, where it
is nighttime, of course. She said a photo of our
daughter will be faxed to us very soon. My heart
has been racing ever since. I'm excited and scared
and then sad remembering my baby will not be
newborn. Two hours after the lawyer called it
dawned on me that we don't have a fax machine.
Willem has a fax machine at work, and if I need
to, I send faxes from the copy store down the street.
If it's sent to Willem's office, his colleagues will see
my child's picture before I do, and I don't want
that. Two people work at the copy store, a beautiful
young woman from Hungary with a tiny ring in
her nose and a young Iranian man who was raised
in India. I have talked to them for several years.
They have Xeroxed all the adoption papers. I do
not know their names, but I like them very much.
I would not mind if they saw a picture of my
daughter before me.

I called Willem at work to tell him about the fax.
He was very quiet.

"This is progress, right?" I said.

"I guess so," he murmured. "I guess so."

I walked down Broadway to the YMCA to teach feeling jubilant. A picture, albeit a grainy picture, would be transmitted across the land and under the Atlantic Ocean from Lithuania, a picture of my daughter. I wondered if she has hair.

October 15, 1995

Today I sorted through the last possible box of papers before we get our daughter. In the back of old calendars I'd kept since I was twelve years old, I found crooked lists of numbers chronicling my menstrual cycle, as if I was looking for some kind of pattern to my life, as carefully attended to as boys' box scores.

October 17, 1995

I went to a pediatrician in the neighborhood to talk. Nowadays people interview doctors, but I always feel I'm the one being interrogated. This physician was a kind, shaggy-looking man, who said that many people in his practice were adopted. Until 1991 he'd mainly seen children from South Korea.

"And now?" I said.

"Vietnam, Thailand, Colombia, Peru, Chile, Paraguay, Costa Rica, Haiti, and lots of little girls from China."

"What about Eastern Europe?"

"Some. More and more. A few from Russia. A few from Romania. If possible we'd like to see medical records before, but they are never reliable. To get the children out they often have to say there's a medical reason when there is not. But of course sometimes there is, so it's hard to know what data is accurate."

"When should I bring the baby in?" I asked.

"Some people come straight from the airport," he answered.

October 18, 1995

This morning, as I made pancakes for Willem, I raised the spatula over the bubbling skillet and recalled a breakfast from thirty-eight years ago. I was seated at the breakfast table in front of a box of cereal. On the back of the box was the most beautiful doll with long blond hair. This was before I could read, and my mother explained that if we sent in the form on the back I could have the doll. I was beside myself. My mother even cut out the coupon while there was cereal in the box. For weeks there was a big gaping spot, revealing the wax paper bag like a skirt with a hole in it showing a white slip. I waited and waited for that doll, and it never arrived. I feel like that's what Willem and I are doing now, but I'm determined for our doll to arrive.

October 19, 1995

I received a listing in the mail of magazines and newsletters about adoption:

Add-Option
Adoptalk
Adopted Child Newsletter
The Adoption Advocate's Newsletter
Adoption Therapist
Adoption Therapy Coalition Journal
Annual Report on Foreign Adoption

The Decree
Face Facts
National Adoption Reports
Reunions
Roots & Wings

and a detailed explanation about finding adoption information on the Internet. I put the envelope in a file and stuffed it in the back of my filing cabinet.

October 23, 1995

I figure my baby must be four months old now if she was born in June. According to *What to Expect Your Baby's First Year*, she should be able to lift her head up 90 degrees, laugh out loud, and follow an object in an arc about six inches above her face for 180 degrees, and she might, among other things, pay attention to a raisin.

This weekend, after many days of snarling at each other, Willem and I fell in love again. We drove on flooded roads to Philadelphia to see the Brancusi show at the Philadelphia Museum of Art. The sky was lit up like a Tintoretto painting and we entertained ourselves by imitating the different sounds animals make in Dutch and in English. In Dutch a cow says "Boo" rather than "Moo," and I can't begin to mimic what Dutch roosters say. I wonder about Lithuanian cows.

October 24, 1995

Yesterday I was feeling fragile as I walked to Central Park to go jogging, as if I might lose my balance any minute, when I bumped into a man I used to go out with years ago. "Adopting?" he said when I shared my news. "She'll be over four months? Isn't that like getting a used car?"

I felt so nauseous at that point, I almost fell over, but all I could do was to scowl at this man as I stood there squinting in the October light. When I escaped as quickly as I could, I managed to jog lamely around the reservoir. On my return from the park, a young, tousled homeless person stood on my corner begging. As I dropped a coin in his cup from my sweat pants pocket, I looked into the young man's eyes, and for a moment I could imagine him when he was a baby. He was surely not

homeless then. He was probably in a tiny baby outfit, clean and warm somewhere else in America.

October 26, 1995

Today I felt so weak I couldn't make myself jog,
but I went for a long walk, kicking through the
leaves in the park. With my head bent, I practically
bumped into a friend of mine with her three children. She had her newborn son in her arms with a
little Cleveland Indians cap on his head. Her two
girls were playing Ring Around the Rosey around
her, and I asked the younger one how old she was.
She proudly held up three fingers. "I'm pretending
to be three," she said. In fact, her mother said, she
was two. At that moment, my loneliness fell away.

October 27, 1995

Yesterday Willem called from work and asked if
I'd like to meet him at the Museum of Modern Art.
I was thrilled. I hadn't been asked out on a date in
a long time. I realized I had been wearing the same

jeans and T-shirt every day for four months, except when I was teaching. Actually I have five T-shirts and three pairs of the same pants, but last night I got dolled up and tried not to worry about whether my baby would burn herself on the bathroom radiator. When I met Willem at the museum I noticed he wasn't wearing a belt, and for a second I was convinced he'd forgotten it at another woman's house.

"Where's your belt?" I whispered subtly after we kissed hello.

"I forgot it this morning. You know."

It was true. European men don't wear belts, and every so often he forgets, just as occasionally he'll talk Dutch to me when he thinks he's talking English.

We went through the Mondrian exhibit, seeing his work go from realistic landscapes to the spare, stylized lines for which he's famous. Even in the photographs of the artist he himself gets more stylized, and his studio is pared down. The catalog stresses the influence of jazz on Mondrian, but if you ask me, who lives with a fellow countryman, his simple no-frills look is straight out of Dutch Calvinism. As we drifted through the museum I remembered a man I had met there and spent far too long with after that, a man who admitted he had wet his pants in kindergarten and told his teacher he didn't do it.

October 30, 1995

Today is my birthday. I am forty-two. We went to the beach over the weekend and ran in the rain and walked on the beach until the sun came out. Today I was drawn like a magnet onto a bus to midtown Manhattan, a place I've tried to avoid for years. I found myself drifting into a department store and wandering around the makeup counters. When I saw a man who seemed to be telling everybody else what to do, I said, "Excuse me, but could you suggest something for you know, under my eyes?"

This man took my elbow in his manicured hand, steered me over to a counter, and handed me a magnifying mirror. Then he took a tiny jar of beige cream and dabbed the wrinkles around my eyes.

"These are for your 'expression lines,'" he said.

The last time I'd undertaken such a project I think the word was "crows' feet."

"Is there anything else I need?" I asked as he frowned and patted another cream on the bags under my eyes.

"Lipstick wouldn't hurt," he said, and took a brush and began dabbing my lips with some pretty shade of red. I did look better.

"Rouge?" he asked. "And a brush. You need a brush."

He continued his artistry as I said, "How much are the brushes?"

"This is squirrel. It's $58. We believe in brushes," he said, and as he applied the rouge I could feel a squirrel tail swish over my face.

I looked pretty good. "I think I'll take the under-eye cream, and the 'crows', I mean the 'expression line' cream, and okay, it's my birthday, the lipstick."

I refrained from the squirrel but walked out with my little bag of cosmetic treats feeling quite grown up. It is sad that I will rarely bring myself to use them.

November 2, 1995

Last night we went to a party and I immediately spied a woman holding a plump and smiling baby. "How old is that baby?" I whispered to Willem.

"Go ask," he said.

After about fifteen minutes I sidled up to the mother and her son. When she told me he was five months old, I blurted out, "We're adopting a baby girl who is five months now."

"Here, hold him to get the feel," she said, handing me her jolly bundle. And then she added, "I was adopted at five months."

At that moment the rest of the party fell away and I fell in love with this woman and her baby. Cradling that sweet baby felt just right.

"Do you have any advice for me?" I asked.

"Be honest," said the woman. "From the moment my mother got me she told me, 'Now, you had a mother who was unable to take care of you, and I was not able to have a baby so it worked out for both of us. We both love you very much.' I always felt it was special to be adopted. I loved telling guys. I somehow felt it was sexy or something."

November 6, 1995

Willem stayed up most of the night watching the news, as I twisted in the bed. *"J'ai passé une nuit blanche,"* as the French say. I had a white night, a sleepless night. Today the cans of baby formula I bought many, many months ago, expired, and I had to take my computer to be repaired. Today is also my mother's parents' anniversary, although my grandfather died seven years ago. They were married for sixty-five years. I went to lunch with my grandmother to celebrate. My grandparents had three close sets of friends who were also married in November. They called themselves the November Club, and every November they took a trip together. "We always treated each other's children like our own," my grandmother said.

November 8, 1995

Last night Willem and I woke up at 3 A.M. again. It turns out that both of us have a wild fear we're going to die before the baby comes. Perhaps we're mourning the end of our childhoods, finally, at forty-five and forty-two.

November 11, 1995

Last night we went to a party and I could not stop telling people we were adopting a baby. I feel like I should be allowed the pleasure of being congratulated, exactly as much as if I were pregnant, but there is a small percentage of people who do not give me the exact response I'm looking for. They are the ones who immediately launch into the most horrendous tales they have heard about adoption when you mention the word. They gasp and say "Oh no," rolling their eyes. "We know someone who adopted and it turned out the birth mother was a crack addict and the birth father kidnapped the baby after the adoption. . . . I'm sure this won't happen to you . . ."

Today was a day of "upsetness," as Kato Kalin would say. I rose early and flicked on my computer, which had just been fixed for a large sum of money, and it did not work. I bent my head down on my desk. I felt exhausted, but Willem kindly offered to drop it at the repair shop on his way to work. It was pouring rain and I had to use my typewriter to write up comments on my students' work, so I was running late and jumped in a cab to get to class.

The driver immediately asked me to guess where he was from.

I shut my eyes and guessed, "India."

"Pakistan," he said. "Do you have any children?" he continued.

"Not yet, my husband and I are adopting a baby."

"Oh, no," he said, swiveling his head around to stare at me. "You must pray all the time. You must pray to Allah."

I arrived at class late and worn out. I was off balance and did not teach well.

When I got home there was a message on the

answering machine from the lawyer to call her immediately. I stood in my dripping wet coat and dialed her number nervously.

"I just got back from Lithuania. The baby has a viral infection," she said. "She's conquered it, but she's still weak. I wasn't allowed into the orphanage to see her."

"How sick? What did she have? What's it called?"

"I don't know the name in English. I'm going to try and get her medical records sent to your pediatrician."

I got off the phone in a stupor. Viral infection could mean anything. A cold, chicken pox, measles, AIDS, what viral infection? How weak is my daughter? I need to see her. "She conquered it?" I mumbled, and fell onto the couch exhausted.

At 6 P.M. I got a call from Willem at the computer store. I decided to wait and talk to him when he got home. "They say you must have dropped the machine," he said quietly into the phone.

"I didn't drop the machine!" I yelled. "I took the computer home, put it on my desk, and it was broken. They were supposed to have repaired it!"

"The guy says a little piece broke off, that you probably bumped it."

"Maybe *they* bumped it!" I screamed. I was "ballistic," an American phrase Willem recently picked up.

"Could I talk to the guy?"

"Yes," said Willem, only too eager not to have my wrath in his ear.

"Hello, this is Ron," the man said.

And then I screamed at him. I told him he was incompetent and I insisted on talking to the manager. The manager had gone home, he said. I could feel my face turn purple, and then I hung up on him.

Willem called back a moment later. "Your computer is in pieces at this point. I don't think you used the best tactics . . ."

When Willem got home, without the computer, I apologized to him and told him about our sick baby. All he said was, "This is crazy."

I tried to make a normal meal, but I forgot to put water in the pot when I steamed vegetables, so the pot and the steamer and the vegetables burned.

I needed to hear Willem talk, but he withdrew

to watch basketball on TV. I wandered around the house thinking: It's winter in Eastern Europe. Our baby is sick. Why don't we have her with us?

I marched in front of the TV and pleaded to Willem, "What should we do?"

"I can't think," he said. "Let's talk about it tomorrow."

I went into the bedroom, slammed the door, and grumbled ungodly things.

November 15, 1995

When I woke up this morning I decided I would call the computer guy and apologize. I decided I would tell him we were adopting a baby and heard disturbing news and that was that. I felt a strong urge to tell the truth. I felt I had to get my priorities straight. When I got up I showered and put on perfume. I made Willem a calm breakfast of eggs, toast, juice and coffee. When the computer service center opened at 10 A.M. I called.

"I would like to talk to Ron," I said.

Ron got on the phone.

"I would like to apologize," I said. "We're adopting a baby and got some upsetting news yesterday—"

"Say no more," he said. "I'm the father of four adopted children."

"I'm sorry for the way I acted."

"No problem," he said. "Ninety-nine percent of our screamers don't apologize."

November 16, 1995

I had a quiet meeting with Ron at the computer repair center. I felt like I was meeting with some kind of guidance counselor. He is a jovial, round-faced man, who sat across from me with my healed computer between us. For thirty minutes we did not discuss the machine. Instead Ron entertained me with dramatic stories of getting his babies out of Bogota. And then he said, there are three unnerving things people often say about adoption: (1) "Do you have any natural children? (2) "Do you have any real children?" (3) "Do you have any children of your own?"

Actually, he used the word "stupid" instead of

unnerving. He also said that as his kids got older sometimes they wanted to talk about the adoption a lot, but then sometimes not at all.

I felt soothed by Ron, and as I left the store, I gently cradled my computer, which I know I did not bump. Out on the street a bus pulled up at the bus stop with a big ad on the side: FIRST TELE-VISED WAR TRIALS SINCE NUREMBERG! WATCH IT DAILY ON COURT TV! What a great show, the trials and tortures of Bosnia. Live from the Hague.

November 17, 1995

The U.S. government is shut down, and on the news they say how sad it is that the national parks are closed and the Vermeer exhibit in Washington is closed, but I frankly don't care about that. The shutdown will delay getting our baby even longer. Our baby cannot get into this country without an immigration visa, but the American embassy in Warsaw will be closed, which means the mess of paperwork will be piling up. All through our wait people have said, "How can you be so patient?" and I've sighed and said, "Things are different in Eastern Europe . . ." but this is our country, the land of the free and the brave. I'm ready to join the Militia.

November 18, 1995

I don't want to tell my friends or family that my baby is sick. Instead I told the woman who works at the cleaners, a woman whose name I do not know. I also rely on the comfort of my students. Their stories filled me up today. They read their tales about humid summers in Dallas, playing field hockey on a German beach before the War, a first refrigerator in a Harlem tenement, meeting Nureyev on a Paris street, springtime in Siberia . . .

November 19, 1995

A package arrived from Holland, as it has every year of our marriage at this time, full of remarkably realistic-looking bananas and sausages and oranges shaped from marzipan, as well as large letters of the alphabet made out of chocolate and *pepernoten* (small pieces of gingerbread), all in honor of Sinterklass, who arrives in Holland from Spain on a ship each year on the evening of December 5 and leaves gifts in the shoes of Dutch children. I stuffed myself with marzipan as I thought of my sick baby. I don't even know where she is now. In the orphanage? In a hospital? What happened to that photograph that was supposed to be faxed under the ocean?

November 20, 1995

We still don't have any medical reports on our daughter, but the American government has re-opened.

Thanksgiving 1995

Thanksgiving has always been too much for me to bear. I think it's why I married a European. I feel weighted down from all the Thanksgivings past, when my parents were married, all those long meals, and then the first years of the divorce . . . The best was a picnic on the beach in Oregon and a Vietnamese meal in Paris. I have no appetite thinking about my sick baby.

November 30, 1995

Another little girl was murdered by her mother in New York. Her bright-eyed face is on the front page of every newspaper and floats across the television screen. Nobody fingerprinted that murderous mother before she had that baby. Now Willem has begun cleaning out closets to calm his nerves. Today he unearthed some games from his childhood, and I can see him as a little boy, on quiet, cold nights in the parsonage, without a television, without videos, playing these games with his three long-legged sisters on the floor.

December 1, 1995

There's an icy wind today, but Willem and I decided to play tennis. We ran to the courts in Central Park and played a set, jumping up and down between serves to keep warm.

And now, my husband is sitting in the kitchen with a woman named Fern, a singer who needs help pronouncing lyrics of Dutch songs for a concert she is giving. Her laugher rises in waves as he translates and tells her how to hold the words in her mouth. Of course the lyrics are full of love and desire. I sit in the office, fuming. I don't want to be the wife. I want to be the single woman laughing in the kitchen with a married man. Fern is wearing lots of scarves and jewelry and high heels with straps. I'm wearing khaki pants and a long-sleeved white T-shirt that is stained from cleaning under the kitchen sink.

December 2, 1995

I've been reading about women who fall in love with men who are in prison. It's a very popular way to fall in love, but it is very rare for men to fall in love with women who are in prison. In fact, very few men even visit women in prison. Visiting days in a women's prison find children and mothers and sisters, but you have to hunt around for the men. I feel like my daughter is in prison and I can't go visit her.

December 11, 1995

A list arrived in the mail from Coleen, who adopted a baby from China. "Thought this might come in handy," she wrote.

nice clothes for court
camera
film
money belt
umbrella (doubles as parasol)
fork, spoon, knife
antibacterial dishwashing liquid
Ziploc bags
toilet paper
ear plugs (so one of you can sleep)
diaper bag (we found a backpack was good for lines
    in airport, embassies, etc.)
wipes
bottles
nipples

formula
Thermos
baby clothes
bibs
toys
pacifiers
blankets
antibiotics for baby
Baby Tylenol
Nix for lice (get family pack)
Eliminate 5% cream for scabies
hydrocortisone cream
bug lotion
sunscreen for infants
antibiotics
Sudafed
Tylenol
Diarrhea/constipation pills
vitamins
document bag
plastic envelopes
passports and visas
INS approval INS1-60A approval and 1171H
INS 230
birth certificates

marriage license
past two years of 1040 forms (2 copies each)
Home Study

Even though we are going to Europe, not China, and will not need some of these things, I could not bear to read this list and stuffed it in the filing cabinet with some of the other adoption information. Instead I read Elizabeth Bishop's letters as pale fog and snow swept across the Hudson.

December 17, 1995

I had my last classes before the holidays. My students baked all kinds of sweets, and I felt nervous eating in front of them, worried that I was teaching with powdered sugar on my lips. I miss my students already: the woman who was once a lonely little girl standing in a windswept yard by the railroad tracks in Nebraska; the woman who had a baby brother who wore glasses tied around his baby head with a pink ribbon, which earned him the name "the professor" before the Nazis took him away; the man from Sapulpa, Oklahoma, whose mother called him Jimmy darling; the nun from Ohio who fled the convent and married and became a psychologist; the woman who lost her high school sweetheart in the Pacific the day after she dreamed he was shot down . . .

Willem and I trade off being angry. He periodically erupts into a tirade at the lawyer and Eastern Europe and I try to calm him down. "That's just the way adoption is. Everybody is doing the best they can," I purr, which annoys him even more. But then I get into a fury, screaming at Newt Gingrich on the television screen. "How can he be *Time* Man of the Year! He caused the government to shut down! He's kept our baby from us!" while Willem quietly tries to watch the news.

December 20, 1995

The lawyer called this evening.

"I have very sad news to tell you," she said hesitantly. "The little girl died. I'm so sorry." Her voice was cracking. "There are several baby boys ready to be adopted now."

I could barely breathe. I pulled the phone away from my ear and watched the snow falling. There are eighteen inches of snow on the ground. I want the snow to keep falling forever.

After I got off the phone I didn't even tell Willem. I wandered in a daze into the baby's room. It doesn't look particularly like a girl's room. There is no pink. In fact, the rug and the curtains are light blue. There are two dolls in the crib but nothing else distinctly female. I opened the closet, which was full of little puffy dresses my sister sent. They hung like cupcakes. One by one I carefully slid each outfit off the little hangers. Then I turned off the light and sat at the window, clutching the clothes, staring at the snow falling on the river. The baby boat took our daughter back.

Winter Solstice. The shortest day. The U.S. government has been closed again, but frankly it's the
least of my concerns right now. Willem and I have
been hugging each other a lot, but we don't know
what to say to each other. I'm numb but still convinced we'll get a baby. He's more skeptical. My
solution today was to trudge to Central Park with
my x-country skis. There was a foot of beautiful
white powder and a handful of people on skis. I
zigzagged along the bridle path. "Next year," I
whispered to myself out in that quiet snow. "Next
winter I'll take my baby in the snow." And then I
said a little prayer for my lost daughter.

December 27, 1995

I could not sleep last night. I lay in bed saying the word "son." I like the word, "sun, son, sun." "Son" is "sound" in French. I said it over and over, "son, son, son." At 5 A.M. I staggered into the baby's room and sat in the dark holding a stuffed teddy bear. How long will the Babar posters be on his wall? I wondered. When will it be full of loud music and gym socks and even *Playboy* magazines hidden under the mattress? I stared out at tugboats strung with Christmas lights gliding up the river.

December 31, 1995

I feel completely alone. I'm in mourning for a baby I never met. I finally had to tell somebody, and I called my father. I could hear him hold back his own tears for his lost granddaughter as he comforted me.

January 1, 1996

I read more letters of Elizabeth Bishop to get me through the day. My favorite image is of her returning to America after living in Brazil and delighting in the food in the big supermarkets. She spent hours in the aisles, reading the elaborate lists of ingredients on the packages, savoring all the words.

We went to a party last night for a few hours, and I was nervous. I couldn't bear to tell people that our little girl died. I couldn't stand to say it out loud and then hear all their questions. When people asked how things were going, I just said, "Things didn't work out with the baby girl. I think we'll be getting a boy." I did meet a woman who was born 300 miles north of the Arctic Circle, the most northern-born person I ever had a conversation with, which was, by its nature, refreshing.

January 4, 1996

Folks, I'm telling you
Birthing is hard
and dying is mean,
So get yourself
a little loving
in between.
—LANGSTON HUGHES

January 5, 1996

Willem and I have gotten back together. To an out-side observer we had never separated, but we do some kind of dance where we spin away from each other, and then, for no reason we can put into words, we spin back into each other's arms. Even if a small team of anthropologists chose to move in with us, I don't believe they could discern the moment when we split apart. Our dance ebbs and flows from sweet intimacy to aching loneliness constantly. And when I feel close to him I have the urge to cook. Today I baked two pies.

January 8, 1996

The second-worst blizzard of the century is wrapping its arms around the city. There are two and a half feet of snow and a piercing wind. Yesterday I spied one lone tugboat plowing through the ice on the Hudson, but today there are no boats. From the sixteenth floor it feels as if we're on top of a blustery mountain.

The government has had the sense to open, but because of the blizzard all government offices remain closed for the day. The mail isn't even being delivered and driving is banned in midtown Manhattan. This afternoon I'll bundle for the cold and attempt to x-country ski in the street. I was supposed to get my hair cut and had the wild urge to bob it short like Audrey Hepburn, but perhaps thankfully, the hairdresser is closed.

Willem just informed me that now there is a basketball player from Lithuania on the Portland Trailblazers. He is 7'3". His name is Arudys Sabonis. I wonder how tall our son will be.

January 10, 1996

Today I was propelled from my desk, through the great drifts of snow to the bookstore. I wandered aimlessly through the shelves, dragging my finger along the spines of the books like a wayward child, and in the foreign language section I landed on a fat Lithuanian dictionary. I carefully took it from the shelf like it was a treasure chest. I opened it carefully and read words I have never seen, words that have never entered my ears.

baby — kudikis
boy — berniukas
love — meile
to be in love with — butisimylejusiam
kiss — bucinys
to kiss one's hand — pasiusti bucini

I felt a rush of excitement, mouthing words that my son might have heard. I bought the dictionary with trembling hands.

January 12, 1996

Last night I dreamed that I had a string around my finger, and at the end of the string was a house in heaven.

As I sipped my tea this morning at breakfast I stared at the front page of the newspaper with a picture of François Mitterrand's large family at his funeral.

"Who is this? His sister?" I asked Willem, pointing to one of the women.

"His mistress," he said. "And a daughter by her."

"Oh," I said, staring out at the snow. "When I die, no mistresses at the funeral."

Yesterday a young, handsome man came to scrape the ceiling where leaks have come through. He was lovely to look at and interesting to talk to. At one point he stood very close to me and we looked out at the roofs across the city. He explained to me how water towers work (not the first man to do so), but he added that there is a trap at the bottom of each building called a "fish trap" to capture any lost fish from the reservoirs, which made me fall in love with him. As much as I loved him I felt confined with him in the apartment, and I wondered if having a child would be like having a construction worker in the house for the rest of my life.

At the end of the day I went with a friend to pick up her daughters after school. I got a headache seeing the mass of children jumping around, which is how I always felt at school. I did like the way the teacher of each class shook each child's small hand to bid them good-bye. I wouldn't mind someone shaking my hand at the end of each day.

When I returned home I got a call from an old friend. "You still haven't gotten your baby yet?" she shrieked. "Don't worry, you'll completely forget this time of your life, completely forget it."

Several people have said that to me, but I don't want to forget this time at all. Nobody says a pregnant woman should forget *her* time of waiting. It's how I'm becoming a mother.

January 13, 1996

The skies are sunny for the first time in days, but the streets and sidewalks are sheeted with ice, and each crosswalk is either a dark moat of icy water or a mountain of snow. I stayed in most of the day and read. My cousin gave me a copy of *Practical Parenting Tips: Over 1500 Helpful Hints for the First Five Years*. I read each page carefully, from birth to sending a child off to first grade. My favorite advice in the whole book was a remedy for removing chewing gum from a child's hair. "Use peanut butter. Work it into hair. Comb out gum and peanut butter."

And the most Zen, which I plan to try on Willem when he gets worked up: "Whisper in his or her ear. Screaming will usually stop and if you can think of something really good to whisper, the child's mood may change."

January 19, 1996

There's a low fog over the Hudson and seagulls are squawking in from the Atlantic. Discarded Christmas trees are stuck in the mounds of snow, lining the streets with evergreens. Today Willem woke up feeling melancholy. It is the anniversary of his mother's death. One morning fifteen years ago when he lived on St. Mark's Place in the East Village, he got the call. He stumbled out of his loft bed to hear the awful news from Amsterdam, that his mother had died suddenly in a store while buying a pair of pajamas.

January 20, 1996

Last night we got the call. Last night we got THE CALL. Last night we got what we hope is the announcement about our baby, our son, our child. The lawyer called at 6:45 P.M., just as we sat down to dinner. We often don't pick up the phone while we're eating, but for some reason I stood and lifted up the receiver.

"Sit down," the lawyer said. "This is it," but I did not sit down. "Do you have a pencil?" she asked, and carefully spelled out the two beautiful Lithuanian names, first and last, of our son. The words sounded like two rivers flowing together, and I knew we finally would be parents.

"The baby was fifty-two centimeters at birth."

I whispered "fifty-two centimeters" to Willem,

and he made a big space between his Dutch hands, which are familiar with centimeters.

"He was born in October," and then she told me his birth date.

"And when can we get him?" I asked calmly.

"Hopefully February," said the lawyer. "Next month."

When I hung up the phone I said the name over and over to Willem. "Isn't it a beautiful name? Our son has a beautiful name."

"When?" Willem said, apprehensively. "What about medical reports?"

"This baby's healthy," I promised. "I know it. This is our son."

All during dinner I chattered away, saying his name, saying his birth date. And then we lit some candles and prayed he would stay healthy. But it was clear Willem was still skeptical. In fact, according to the car-crash law, we both knew we wouldn't be going to Lithuania in February. We both knew there would be a delay.

I couldn't sleep a wink last night as I calculated where I had been on the day of my son's birth. It was a hot summer day in autumn. I don't want to tell anybody my son's lilting Lithuanian name. We'll give him an American name, which is the same as Willem's favorite soccer player, favorite philosopher, and favorite singer, but his Lithuanian name, his birth name, will be his to share with people when he's ready.

January 23, 1996

Last night I drove to an open house at a college where I'll be teaching. There was a panel of teachers and a crowd of students. These things are often a strange kind of battle of the bands, with nervous teachers trying to make their workshops sound like the greatest thing since Cracker Jack. I was exhausted all day worrying about it, but it turned out to be a friendly group, all of us teachers coming out of our caves for the occasion.

On the drive back to the city in the dark I was comforted by the majestic arcs of the George Washington Bridge, as I have been since I was a child and my mother drove my brother and sister and me into "the City" to the Museum of Natural

History. We always had to get dressed up, and I often had to wear white gloves. I used to love to stand up in the back, before seat belts of course, and pat my mother's beautiful auburn hair. And there was always a fleeting moment when she'd say "Watch for the Little Red Lighthouse, children," and we'd crane our necks and for a split second, a magic moment, we'd see the lighthouse, just like in our story book, standing proudly under the bridge.

January 24, 1996

Yesterday I went swimming to clear my head and there was one of my men students hoisting his old athlete's body out of the water. J. B., he signs his stories, and he is a passionate, talented, wild man, and I was ashamed to have him see me in my bathing suit and ashamed to see him in his. We joked about writing and swimming briefly, both of us awkwardly trying to stand at ease in our exposed bodies. We bid each other good-bye and I slid into the pool. Halfway through my laps I lifted my head to do a turn and saw J. B, in his clothes now, returning to the pool. He was waving an envelope. I stopped swimming and lifted my bathing cap from my ear to hear what he was saying.

"This is for you," he called, and tucked the envelope in a stack of kickboards by the edge of the pool.

I smiled and waved back. What was this? A billet-doux? I'd never gotten a letter in the middle of swimming. I dutifully finished my laps and pulled myself out of the pool. I dried myself, then gingerly opened the envelope. It was a poem, a poem about a mother and a baby he had written. It was the best baby present so far.

January 25, 1996

In President Clinton's State of the Union Address he vowed not to close the government down again, and Willem and I stood up in the living room and clapped and cheered, just like the members of Congress did. I'm getting excited about our son, but I sense that something sad will happen at the same time. Willem and I are reading Toni Morrison's *Beloved* aloud to each other, and at the start of the book she says the grandmother dies "soft as cream." I don't want to lose anybody in my family, but the thought of the arrival of our child also brings an uneasiness to my soul. I pray my loved ones die "soft as cream."

I looked up two new words in the Lithuanian dictionary: fear—baime and worry—nerimas.

January 29, 1996

I'm sleeping less and less at night, and at strange points during the day I throw myself down on the bed diagonally in a vain attempt to rest. I remember my mother lying diagonally on the bed occasionally during the day when I was a child and I was always so startled to see her there. I also have a curious urge to make flour-and-water paste, like my mother used to, so my brother and sister and I could make paper collages on the kitchen table.

I received an Emily Dickinson poem in the mail
from a friend who just lost someone dear to her.

> She went as quiet as the dew
> from a familiar flower.
> Not like the dew did she return
> at the accustomed hour!
> She dropped as softly as a star
> from out my summers eve;
> less skillful than Leverrier
> It's sorer to believed.

I had to go to the encyclopedia to look up Lever-
rier, who was a nineteenth-century astronomer. I
hope my little girl went "as quiet as the dew." They
say that if you share your sorrow, people will comfort you, but I've never been good at that. I did get
a card that said "Your sponsored foster child was
born on March 18, 1987, and will be celebrating
her birthday soon," and so I sent her a card, another faraway child, and that made me feel better.

February 1, 1996

Michael Jordan is back playing basketball after following his baseball dream, and seeing his smile and watching him score nineteen points lifted Willem's spirits and mine as well. "Next winter," I told Willem, "you'll have a son to watch these games with."

Construction workers are here for the next four days, tending to the leaks in the ceiling. The men's names are Demetrius and Bill. Bill appears to be twenty years older than Demetrius. One day when I was a child, two strong men came to do some construction work on our house and while they ate their salami sandwiches I sat in the leaves at their feet as if they were gods. Then they asked me to play football with them. They got a football from the back of their pickup truck, and as we threw it back and forth I was in ecstasy. Before I could object, the one with the dark curly hair and muscled arms bent down and put his hands on my shoulders to form a miniature huddle. "Okay," he whispered, "we'll do a Statue of Liberty play," and he lightly drew the play on my shirt with one finger, just under my neck, along my collar bone. To this day, it was the most sensual experience of my life.

Odds are that I will not be playing football with Demetrius and Bill, although the apartment does smell of sweat, which I like.

February 2, 1996

The groundhog saw its shadow, so there will be six more weeks of this record-breaking winter this year.

February 3, 1996

We received a letter from a friend in Holland. She and her husband have two children, a son and a daughter. Their daughter was adopted. "Being a mother is the same for both my children," wrote our friend. "At first, whenever my daughter had a problem I would think, was it because she's adopted? But it doesn't matter why. What matters is, they are our children."

February 4, 1997

We went to an exhibit of the Brontës and for fifteen minutes we were alone in a room full of Charlotte's kid gloves, tiny stones Anne had collected on the beach, watercolors of birds by poor brother Branwell, and the tiny books, 2,500 microscopic words per page, about toy soldiers that they wrote as children in the parsonage.

February 6, 1996

I am jubilant. Bill and Demetrius finished plastering and painting and the apartment is a fresh, clean place. When they left, Bill gave me his card and his name is not Bill at all, he explained. It is Vasilios, and he is Demetrius's father, but after twenty years in this country he is weary of repeating his real name. After they left I found some newspapers on the floor and my eye caught a picture of Clinton holding a baby. The caption said "Clinton dandles baby." Dangle? Handles? I looked it up and learned it meant "to rock or cradle a baby." I can't wait to dandle my baby.

February 8, 1996

Willem brought home a video on the Baltics from the public library, and we sat watching a section on Lithuania, squinting to see if we could see our baby, straining to see what he will look like. In 1991 citizens of Lithuania, Latvia, and Estonia held hands in a human chain across all three countries as a symbol of liberation from the Russians. Were the parents of our baby in that human chain?

February 16, 1996

I gave my students the assignment to write about a memory of a car, and one woman wrote about her brother who was killed in an accident forty years ago when he stopped to help someone change a tire. The woman began to cry as she read the piece. I offered to read the rest of it for her. She handed me the paper and I read how nobody in her family had been able to say the brother's name since the accident. The piece ended with the sentence "His name was Francis," and I had to hold back my own tears.

February 25, 1996

It's a strange balmy day, with a fierce blue sky and fifty-mile-an-hour winds, and we certainly don't appear to be going to Lithuania this month. There are whitecaps on the Hudson that we can see from our window, making us long for the open road. With the car blowing back and forth we headed to West Orange, New Jersey to visit Thomas Alva Edison's laboratory and home. Alva, as he was called, was featured on one of Willem's videos he brought home from the library and watched after I went to sleep. Some men watch porn. Willem watches travel videos. I can't complain. Edison's lab, and his desk left just as it was when he died, full of cigars and test tubes and papers, was extraordinary. He called his workers his "muckers," and he was the chief mucker. I am fascinated by people who are guides, and this particular man closed his eyes each time he said Edison's name, as if he worshiped the man. He spoke reverentially of Edison's eighty-hour work week as he pointed to his cot in the corner of the office. Then we went to the Edison home, a majestic mansion on a hill. Mrs. Edison liked to call herself a "house executive" rather than a housewife, and Edison called his lab his "work-bench" and his home his "thought bench." On both tours, the guides pointed out that only one of Edison's six children bore children. Was there an infertility problem? Did five of them not want children? Neither guide gave a clue. But then, if your father invented the electric light, the phonograph, *and* the movie camera, and if Orville Wright, Helen Keller, and Henry Ford came a-calling, maybe it was just enough for the Edison kids to get through their own lives, without adding babies to the mix.

February 27, 1996

It's been almost eighteen months since we began this adoption process, the equivalent of two pregnancies. I feel as if I'm suspended in midair. In the New York *Times* today, there is an article about a scientific analysis of laughing. It says that children laugh on an average of three hundred times a day.

February 28, 1996

The swans are back in the reservoir in Central Park and I can hear chickadees at the window. There is a thread of spring in the air after the harsh winter, and for the first time in years I miss having a garden. The last time I had one was twenty-one years ago. When I was a student at the University of Oregon it was possible to rent garden space for ten dollars a year. The land was a bicycle ride out of town, and I'd go there every day after classes in spring, with my gardening tools in my bike basket, riding through the soft rain. There were three hundred plots on rich fertile farmland. I planted crooked rows of lettuce and carrots and beans and tomatoes, but other gardeners were more focused. On one side of me an old man planted a whole bursting crop of okra, nothing else, and on the other side was an engineering student who gave me rides on his motorcycle and used a tape measure between each seed. Lettuce, tomatoes, and herbs, that's all he planted. "Fresh salad, every day, that's my goal," he said. As a child I grew pumpkins every year, but now on the sixteenth floor I have to dip my hands in the potted plants to feel the earth.

February 29, 1996

It's Leap Year, Sadie Hawkins Day. When I was thirteen years old, I invited my true love to the Sadie Hawkins Dance. He had a beautiful twin sister, and their parents were from Spain. I loved this boy, with his sad, dark eyes and olive skin, but he would not slow-dance with me. We fast-danced, as we called it then; that he would do with me. And then some years ago I heard he died of AIDS.

March 10, 1996

Yesterday I spent the whole day reading *Snow Falling on Cedars*, which I could not put down. Willem endlessly read the newspaper. He never discusses what is in the newspaper, but occasionally, wordlessly, he gets up, walks to the kitchen cabinet and takes out a scissors, then silently clips out an article.

I once gave the assignment of a memory of a news-paper to my students, and one woman started her piece with "My husband took a large scissors with him when we went on our honeymoon."

March 11, 1996

Laura, my friend who adopted a child on her own, called to see how I was doing. "Remember, if your marriage doesn't work, you can always adopt on your own," she assured me. "A lot of marriages crash during the adoption process. Call the Committee for Single Adoptive Parents. They're in Maryland."

I thanked her, then met my grandmother for lunch. Afterward she wanted to buy me something. This ritual has gone on for forty years. And if I object, she always says I should give her the pleasure of giving me something. Today she bought me a scarf. When I asked about her marriage to my grandfather, she smiled and said, "We had good decades and we had decades that were a bit more difficult."

March 17, 1996

It's a cold and sunny St. Patrick's Day. When I got in the elevator a woman who's been waiting for a baby from China waved a small photo of a wide-eyed child in front of me. "Look at my baby!" she shouted. "I'm going in April!" I do not know this woman's name, and I'm not a natural hugger, but I threw my arms around her.

March 22, 1996

Last night I read Betty Jean Lifton's *Journey of the Adopted Self*, which is a wonderful book, but I can't handle worrying about how my child is going to experience a lack of identity and rage at both the birth mother and me. At this point I just want to cuddle my baby.

March 23, 1996

When I returned yesterday from my endless errands where I accumulated yet another new supply of sponges and paper towels, there was a message in rapid Dutch on the machine. I could tell, from the tone of his sister's voice, that it was grave news. When Willem got home from work last night he listened to it. Cancer. His father has pancreatic cancer. It was too late to call Holland, which is six hours later.

March 24, 1996

Willem didn't sleep last night and at 4 A.M. called his sister. We can't figure out if we should go to Holland right away, or maybe we should stop in Holland on the way back from Lithuania. How long will his father live? And of course, when in fact are we going to get our son? Willem is more silent than usual. He does not want to be comforted. The Hyakutake Comet passed overhead, and we saw its bright light even in the city. It won't be back for four hundred years. What does it portend? The loss of a father? The arrival of a child?

March 25, 1996

My mother visited from Washington and we visited her mother, my grandmother. As we greeted one another I had the sense that we were like those wooden Russian dolls that fit neatly inside one another, and I wondered if they were disappointed that I did not have a child inside of me.

March 26, 1996

Willem and I are exhausted. He came home on Sunday afternoon with his left hand dripping blood. He had been playing field hockey in the Bronx, which he loves to do, with his Dutch team. All had gone well until somehow he got smacked in the hand with someone's stick. We spent four hours in the emergency room. It was overflowing with people who sat dazed, bruised, fevered, and demented, staring at a golf tournament on a television set hanging from the ceiling. After two hours I asked the security guard if we could please watch something else. He kindly climbed up on a counter and switched the channel to *My Fair Lady*. Two hours later, just as Rex Harrison had the sense to fall in love with Audrey Hepburn, Willem's name was called. The physician, a young man from Pakistan, sewed fifteen stitches into his right hand.

When we got home I made pancakes and our conversation was a weary jumble of his banged-up hand, how long his father had to live, and when on earth would we get our baby.

March 27, 1996

My sister turns thirty-nine today and I wish we were closer, like when I learned to drive at fourteen and sat on a phone book to see over the steering wheel. For some reason my parents let me drive her down the driveway to the mailbox and we felt like we were going to the moon. Yesterday, walking home from teaching, I felt a moment of joy seeing a burst of green leaves on a tree on West End Avenue. Only when I was right under it did I realize the leaves were glued on. It's too early for real ones. Barbra Streisand was filming a movie.

March 30, 1996

Molly and Jack are visiting from Texas on their way to the Canary Islands, where the guidebook says it is "eternally spring." Molly and Willem remind me of each other, two people in my life I've played field hockey with. She is an ER doctor and I liked watching her examine the stitches on his wounded hand. I'm glad they get along, but it does not feel like a holiday to me. My mind jumps to Willem's father, who is seventy-three, and to my son, who soon will be six months old. In everything I've read, it says that after a child is over six months old, it will be difficult for him to form close bonds.

Last night I got up at 1 A.M. and Willem was not in bed. I went into the kitchen and saw him looking at our medical encyclopedia, solemnly tracing a picture of the pancreas with his finger, like it was a country on a map.

April 1, 1996

We took Molly and Jack to the airport yesterday. On the way we had a lively discussion about religion. They are not believers, though Molly was raised Catholic and Jack is Presbyterian, but in their Texas neighborhood they are surrounded by churchgoers. The church is the social life. If my son's birth parents are Catholic, what should we raise him as? What is our obligation to him and to his soul?

April 2, 1996

I miss Molly and Jack. Sometimes I wake up in the middle of the night and miss Americans. Yesterday, when they were here, I looked at Willem and realized I had never seen him go to the refrigerator, open the door, and look in with longing, which all my American boyfriends used to do. Willem did not even grow up with a refrigerator. His mother parceled out just enough food for everybody each day, and saying "I'm hungry" was considered a sin. Only starving people were considered hungry.

Today we got a letter from our foster child in India.

Dear Foster Parents,

Good morning. As your loving foster child is not known to write, the village animator writes that the foster child and all others in the family are doing well. They are eager to know about all of your well-being. Hope your foster child will letter to you sooner by her own hand. Sooner, they will grandly celebrate the Pongal festival. On that day they will draw colorful rangoli designs in front of their house and wear new dress material happily. On the second day festival, they will decorate their cattles with paint, balls and balloons. They will eat variety of dishes with mutton items happily. They express their sweet Pongal greetings to you all.

All day I've chanted over and over "sweet Pongal greetings to us all," and it has comforted me.

The lawyer just called and said she is trying to get our court date for a week from tomorrow.

Stop newspaper delivery
Ask Bob to water plants and pick up mail
Tell students I'm going
Finish reading student work

Get Pampers

Get Baby

April 3, 1996

I took three baths today. I just read a book that said Bonnard's wife used to take three baths a day, so Willem has begun calling me Madame Bonnard. I spoke to my sister and she said her younger son was crying because he wanted shoes just like his older brother, not just the same style but the same size! I understand that boy, wanting his brother to be his twin. My sister is excited to be an aunt, and even though she already sent me a box of little girl clothes, she will send another box of her sons' old clothes.

April 4, 1996

The Unabomber has been caught. He's a Harvard graduate. When people ask what we know about our baby's birth parents, I want to say, What difference does it make? I could give birth to a son, send him to Harvard, and he could end up the Unabomber. Ron Brown was killed in a plane crash in Croatia. Mad cow disease is spreading hysteria over England and millions of cows will be slaughtered. The Freemen are holed up in a cabin in Montana. I feel like my son is in a little cocoon in the orphanage.

Easter Sunday

Last night I had two dreams. I dreamed Frank Sinatra drove us to the airport to pick up our baby, and I dreamed our baby was wearing a little baseball hat when we met him. When we took off the hat there was writing in tiny print inside, around and around in circles, just like in the Brontës' little books. The writing in the baseball hat contained everything we would ever need to know about our son.

Unfortunately, I have no idea what it said.

April 9, 1996

Last night it snowed. Willem said "Sweet April has a white hat," which is some kind of a Dutch expression. The Freemen, with their artillery and antigovernment pamphlets, are still holed up in a cabin in Montana. It has been eighteen days. We do not appear to be on a plane to Lithuania. Today I bought a small light-blue baby brush and comb at the drugstore for my son, but I have no idea if he has hair.

April 12, 1996

I just got off the phone with the Lithuanian consul, a patient man with a beautiful accent, who explained that it would be a few more weeks before we would be allowed to get our baby. Apparently there was a scandal recently, not the first. An infant was taken illegally from a mother, and since then the newspaper has been full of articles against foreign adoption. May, I'd settle for a May baby. Springtime in the Baltics sounds fine with me.

April 14, 1996

It is a sweet rainy spring day, and I put away all the tiny baby clothes we've received and the Snuggli, which I'd planned to bring to Lithuania. Our son will be too big at this point for it. Instead, we'll bring a stroller or a backpack. Or maybe he'll be walking by the time we go. Maybe we should bring him a pair of Roller Blades.

April 15, 1996

A pouring-rain-down day. "It is raining pipe stems," as the Dutch say. I feel like Willem is stretched beyond possibility, with a son he's never met in Lithuania and an ailing father in the Netherlands. At times he's been very affectionate lately, but other times he has a kind of loose-limbed frantic energy, madly reorganizing his files, staying up far past midnight, getting overwrought when the Knicks win or lose.

April 18, 1996

It snowed yesterday in Eastern Europe. When the weatherman on CNN does the foreign weather, he sweeps his hand over Europe in about half a second, which is half a second more than any of the other channels, but France, Germany, Poland, Russia, all blur together and we get a glimpse, just a glimpse of what the heavens are throwing down on our child.

April 20, 1996

Old boyfriends are calling. They do every spring, like the swallows returning to Capistrano. Most of the ones who call have not married. There is a loneliness in their voices. It's not that they want me. It's just that longing, that American boy longing of looking into the refrigerator late at night.

April 22, 1996

We went to the beach for the weekend and walked on the sand and breathed the salty air and fell back together again. Willem finally slept through the night. By the end of the weekend he had decided to visit his father. I am not going with him. It is a Dutch trip. His father will not have the energy to talk English, and Willem shouldn't have to worry about translating for me. When Willem called him early this morning he said to his father in Dutch, "Would you like a neighborly visit?" using a very old-fashioned horse-and-buggy term, and his father said it would be wonderful. When Willem got off the phone he smiled the biggest smile I've ever seen from him.

April 24, 1996

The New York *Times* has reported that high school boys are refusing to take showers after gym class. "Too embarrassing," they say. One explanation is that U.S. children have more privacy, fewer siblings, more space of their own at home. I think of my son in the orphanage, so used to having other babies around, all his buddies, boys and girls together, eating and gurgling, crying and bathing together.

April 26, 1996

Willem has flown to Holland and I am reading my students' work, about Shirley who came to New York as a refugee from Germany and found work in a lipstick factory, sticking tiny paper labels on the bottoms of lipstick cases. Janet wrote of picking strawberries warm from the sun as a child in Massachusetts. Sandra wrote of her mother who had terminal cancer but insisted on getting her driver's license renewed. Darlene had a piece about sitting at her aunt's knee as she sewed costumes for showgirls at the Apollo Theater in Harlem.

May 3, 1996

Willem is back from his trip, exhausted but glad he went. Five years ago we were on our three-day honeymoon on a small Dutch island in the Caribbean called St. Eustatius. Willem read a lot, mainly a thick book on World War II. One day I felt the need for more conversation and wandered to the front desk. There was an attractive woman in her sixties working there. We began talking about books, and ten minutes into our talk she said, "When I was eighteen I fell in love, but my fiancé was killed in a car crash. I decided to take driving lessons so I could kill myself as well. But," she said with a giggle, "I fell in love with the driving instructor."

She was still married to the driving instructor, and they ran the hotel where we stayed. I immediately ran back to the room and interrupted Willem's reading to tell him this fascinating tale. This pattern—the interrupting of his reading with something I urgently must tell him—is pretty much a constant pattern in our marriage, as he would attest.

Most of my women students over sixty-five have stayed in their marriages. Many of those in their early fifties are divorced. I can't tell which ones are happier. The younger ones are often more physically active, kayaking and trekking and leaping on trampolines, but not necessarily more at peace. The younger ones expect more of men.

May 6, 1996

I suggested my students write about memories of radio. A number of them wrote that they never switched the channel once a show was selected, that often the whole family listened together and they did not eat or speak during a radio show. One woman, now in her eighties, said that when the radio was introduced, her father was not impressed. "It will never catch on," he said. He did not allow one of the newfangled inventions in the house.

May 9, 1996

Last night Willem sat up very late, carefully putting together paper models of a narrow Dutch house and of the Van Gogh Museum. Years ago I had another boyfriend who stayed up making paper airplanes.

May 12, 1996 Mother's day

Willem is off playing field hockey, I am writing more baby announcements to send off when we return from Lithuania. I know I'm being bold by doing this, and Willem thinks it's bad luck. Of course I should wait until we have our baby in hand, but I have faith that we will soon. It's more than that. I believe I have some effect on getting our son by doing such tasks. And so I write steadily, if a bit unevenly, With great joy we welcome, With great joy we welcome . . . With great joy we welcome . . . With great joy we welcome . . . and then I've written the name we will give our son and his birth date of last year.

I just went out to get some food to make pancakes for Willem when he gets home, and on the way out of the store I gave some change to a man with an outstretched hand. "Happy Mother's Day," he said, which is the first time in my life anybody has ever said this to me. I know we'll get our baby soon.

May 13, 1996

The lawyer called last night from Lithuania. It was three o'clock in the morning her time. She asked us to fax her a document giving her Power of Attorney for one last paper, which we did this morning.

May 14, 1996

The lawyer called again from Lithuania. I was home alone. She said we will fly to Warsaw on Sunday the nineteenth, arrive in Warsaw Monday morning, and then fly on to Vilnius, Lithuania, that afternoon. She has made reservations for us on LOT Polish Airlines. It's the quickest and cheapest way to go. Next Monday we will meet our son.

"Thank you, thank you for calling," I said. "Thank you very much."

When I hung up I called Willem at work and whispered the news to him, and he whispered back "Happy Mother's Day."

It is a record-breaking day in the hot, sticky nineties, and we fly this evening to Warsaw. We have our son's name, but we have no medical report and we have no photograph. Willem is edgy, and when I proclaim my love for this baby he admits that he might not fall in love with him instantly. "I know, I know," I say. "But he's wonderful. You'll see."

In the midst of our packing we had the urge for pancakes and had about fifteen syrupy minutes of calm before the kitchen sink began to leak. For once I knew my priorities. I was not going to think about the sink again. I left a note for the superintendent, and if the whole apartment washes away in the month we're gone, we'll deal with it when we get back.

We took an oppressively hot cab to the airport, with the seats filled with bags of baby clothes and

Pampers. We sat for an hour in traffic on the Triborough Bridge and I thought Willem was going to kill either me or the driver. I tried to calm myself by chanting silently "Sweet Pongal Wishes, Sweet Pongal Wishes, Sweet Pongal Wishes."

The Polish Airline Terminal was packed with people. I scanned the seats to see if we could find our twins, two other middle-age people, an American and a Dutchman, going to Lithuania to find their baby, but I saw no mirror images. There were Americans going on a tour, Poles going home for the summer, and what looked to be a group of Christian Fundamentalist college students. I shut my eyes and could see my great-grandparents arriving at Ellis Island from Poland at the end of the last century. Tomorrow we will meet our son. He is seven months old. "Laba dienas kudikis, Laba dienas kudikis, hello baby, hello baby," I'll say to him.

On the plane I plan to read *The Cloister Walk* about Kathleen Morris's monastic experiences, and Willem has brought back issues of *Jewish Week*.

May 20, 1996

I did not read a word or sleep a wink on the plane. We touched down early this morning in Warsaw in a misty rain, but we did not go into the city. We spent our three-hour layover at the airport before we flew Lithuanian Airlines to Vilnius. The airport did not seem extremely foreign, except the arrivals and departures were all in Polish and the place was full of serious people smoking cigarettes. Over the sound system Cher was singing "It's in His Kiss" very loudly in the cafeteria as we ate sausages and scrambled eggs. I think I was in a trance. I sat watching the bags, staring out at the rainy runways as Willem went to the exchange to get Lithuanian money, litas, and some Polish zlotis for the few days we'll spend in Poland on our return and to the gift shop to find maps of Vilnius and Warsaw.

By the time we boarded the Lithuanian airplane I was having an out-of-body experience. The plane itself was from another world, an old Russian-made military-looking aircraft like I'd seen only in very old black-and-white movies. The stairs went up the back of the plane, like entering into a cave. I banged the stroller up the steps as if I'd done it a million times. Here we go again, going to get our baby in the Baltics. There were only three other people, who looked like businessmen in 1950s-style suits, on the plane. The hour flight was bumpy, and the stewardess spoke only in Lithuanian and Polish so if she had given us directions to jump out the window I would not have understood. I was dizzy with excitement and had to make my way to the bathroom. I felt compelled to see myself in the mirror, but the light was broken. I could discern that the toilet had a wooden seat. We were served sausage, again, and thick bread, and vodka was available, which we probably should have drunk. On the flight I brushed my hair six times to look beautiful for my son. In fact, I imagine I looked like a frazzled grandmother.

We touched down in Lithuania at 4 P.M. It is one hour later than Polish time, and it was rainy and dark. This was not the hot springtime we had left. I was nervous, in a pure, nervous state, whereas Willem seemed strangely calm and deliberate as he gathered his things and we made our way down the aisle. The arrivals terminal looked more like a bus station than an airport, and I now felt I was in a foreign land. Lithuanian sounded like beautiful birds to me. We were told by the lawyer that we would be met by a Polish man named Julius. That was all we knew. "He'll recognize you," she said. A childless couple with a month's worth of luggage and a stroller would be the tipoff. In fact, Julius was there, a jovial man with a strong grip, who shook our hands, grabbed our bags, and tried to hurry us through the customs gate. I went first, tripping on the loose awning of the stroller. Julius was talking to me quickly, saying we'd go straight to the orphanage, and I was nodding, but when we turned to look for Willem, he wasn't there. He had been stopped at the gate. Julius went to see what the problem was, leaving me to wait for the rest of our bags at the empty conveyor belt, which was noisily spinning around. The problem was, Willem needed a visa because he had a Dutch passport, something we had checked on before we left but were given "incorrect information" about. With the help of Julius, who talked quickly in Polish and some Lithuanian to the guards, Willem was able to pay in Lithuanian litas, four to a dollar, the fifteen-dollar fine. He was given a rough piece of paper that looked like an old receipt from a diner, but it would last only for ten days and we needed to be there for a month. The new law stated that we would have to stay in the country a month after we went to court, an appeal period during which the birth parents could still change their minds.

It was five in the evening now, cold and raining, and we were on a wild taxi cab ride, racing to the orphanage to meet our son. Julius sat in the front seat and spoke to the driver while Willem and I clutched each other's hands in the backseat.

After fifteen minutes we entered the city, which even in the rain I could see was a blend of beauty and confusion, a mix of stark Soviet apartment buildings melded with medieval cobblestones and churches. Tina Turner was pumping out a litany of love on the radio as the driver continued to race through the slick streets. Ten minutes later we were heading out of town again, up a hill with lush trees, and then we made an abrupt turn onto a road with no discernible sign. A few more minutes and he pulled in the gravel driveway of a low, pale-yellow brick building.

"Palau," Julius told the driver. He leaned over the seat and told us in English, "I asked him to wait."

"Palau," we mumbled back, but we didn't move,

because we didn't know what we were supposed to do.

"The orphanage. This is it. We'll go in, meet your baby, then the driver will take you to your hotel."

We entered the orphanage through such a low door that Willem had to bend his head, then stepped into a cold, dark hallway. We followed Julius, who had obviously trod these floors before, up two flights of stairs. We could hear the chatter of children and someone talking Lithuanian very loudly on a telephone. Suddenly a woman appeared wearing a long cotton dress and a bandanna. "Please," she said, pointing to a room off the hallway. Willem and I went in as Julius disappeared to deal with the authorities. We were in a small room with two worn red couches and a set of shelves that was bare except for a lone Miss Piggy doll. A crucifix was the only ornamentation on the walls. We sat quietly for fifteen minutes waiting for our baby. We did not speak. I had the urge to brush my hair again, but refrained.

And then a nurse brought in a startlingly beautiful baby, swaddled in a red outfit, with chubby cheeks and a bright smile, and he reached out his arms. I reached for him and cradled my plump son. Willem and I took turns holding him, as the nurse sat on the opposite couch smiling and nodding.

This moment I had waited so long for was like hearing a bell ring a perfect chime. It was not like fireworks. It was a feeling of fullness. "Here you are, little boy," I whispered. "I've been looking all over for you." It was a deep sense of finding someone whom I'd lost for a very long time.

After ten minutes the nurse stood up and held out her arms and we understood we had to give our son back to her. We knew this was the procedure. Tomorrow we will go to court, and then we will have to wait a month, and only then will we be able to take him home. We kissed our son good night and promised to be back in the morning, and he smiled. We have a jolly, little boy. I missed him immediately.

The taxi driver did "palau" (wait) for us, and again we were hurtling through the rainy city, this time with Michael Jackson pounding in our ears. Julius was giving us details about what time we would appear in court and what papers to bring and how to respond to certain questions, but all I could say over and over was "He's so beautiful, he's so beautiful," and Willem could not stop grinning.

We were dropped at the Lietuva Hotel (Lietuva is the Lithuanian word for Lithuania), a Russian-built structure considered one of the fancy hotels for foreigners. Our room had two narrow nun beds pressed to opposite sides of the wall. I ran a bath of lukewarm rusty water and sat in it trying to remember the smell of the back of my son's neck, as Willem sat on one of the nun beds studying the map of Vilnius.

Julius had told us there was a restaurant on top of the hotel, but first we needed to breathe some Lithuanian air. We went back down to the lobby and out into the light rain falling on this ancient city. Willem guided me through old streets overlooking the Neris River, and as usual I had to hurry to keep up with his long strides. I was in a daze, remembering the softness of my baby's hands, when a cluster of girls in long white communion dresses came running past us. They headed into a church and we followed them. Fatigue and incense overtook me as strains of "Gloria in excelsis deo" filled the packed pews. I turned to look up at Willem and saw that he was singing softly.

May 21, 1996 5 A.M.

I can't sleep. I'm sitting in the empty bathtub so I won't wake Willem. The bathroom is brown-and-white tile, "Russian style," says the guidebook. I'm all jazzed up. I have the same wild energy I had as a child when I was going to be in a school play the next day. Last night we had dinner in the restaurant on top of the hotel—lots of shredded carrots and sausages in a room with walls of mirrors and a strobe light spinning colors. The music from *Dirty Dancing* was playing on a scratchy sound system. Willem and I toasted our son with Lithuanian beer. Everything seemed surreal but right. I'm nervous about court. The baby will not be there. I had thought he would. Willem is preoccupied with his visa problem. We shoved the nun beds together and had more passion than we'd had in years. Then we watched Tom Brokaw on CNBC who said that it was the fifty-seventh day of the Freemen's standoff in Montana. Montana feels very far away.

May 22, 1996

I have a stomachache and a headache. It's another cold, rainy day. My soul doesn't seem to have caught up with my jet-lagged body. We had a full schedule yesterday. First we spent an hour in the Latvian embassy, after racing around to three other embassies, because for some reason they would issue Willem a visa for all the Baltic countries for the next month. Now Willem wants to travel to Estonia and Latvia. He is excited about the baby, but he says that while we're here we should see everything we can. I politely pointed out that seeing Russian Orthodox churches and Holocaust memorials are just about the furthest thing from my mind right now.

After the Latvian embassy, Julius took us back to the orphanage. Our vocabulary has now expanded from "hello," to "wait" in Lithuanian. This time Willem asked the taxi driver to "palau."

There are one hundred children in this orphanage, one of the few in Lithuania. We followed a nurse down a hallway into one of the playrooms, a cheerful, bright room with mobiles hanging from the ceiling. There was a large, raised playpen, waist high to a grown-up, and I quickly searched to see if our son was one of the three babies crawling around. He wasn't there and for a second I thought I didn't recognize him, but then a nurse brought him to us. Today he was in light-green pajamas and again he reached out his hands. This time, as he snuggled in my arms, I could feel how big he is. He's nine kilos, 2.2 pounds per kilo, almost twenty pounds. As I rocked back and forth with him in my arms I tried to ask the nurse what he ate, making chewing sounds with my mouth and some kind of "yum-yum" sound. Finally a woman who spoke English came in and translated for us. She held up five fingers and said, "Milk, kasha, milk, kasha, milk." That's all that's touched my son's sweet lips in seven months. Willem and I took turns carrying him around, cooing and talking to him, and to the other little children who waddled up to us. Then the nurse pulled lightly on my sleeve and I followed her into one of the sleeping rooms, another bright, clean room with skylights and six little cribs. Each crib had a huge down pillow in it that Americans would feature on a talk show about the dangers of suffocation and thick down comforters. I definitely had the sense that we were being observed as much as we were observing. As I held our son I felt I was being watched to see if I was a worthy parent. In America the press makes Eastern Europe and their orphanages seem as if they should be thrilled to have us as parents, but here I sense the great pride the Lithuanians have in their children. Now the nurse was pointing at our baby's crib, and I understood it was morning nap time. I could have used a nap myself, but we had to go to court.

Julius took us back to our hotel where we changed into better clothes. Willem put on a tie and jacket, and I got myself into a slightly wrinkled long skirt. Then Julius took us to the center of the city, to a bustling, smoky café for blinis and sour cream that tasted like ambrosia. MTV was on the television above the bar. There were students with punk haircuts and tight jeans and University of Texas sweatshirts chattering in Lithuanian. I've never heard anything like this language. It sounds different from Polish or Russian, which I don't understand either, but I recognize.

"KGB," said Julius, above the music. "The court is in the old KGB building. Just answer the questions the judge asks you. Don't say anything else. It will take about a half hour, then he will decide whether you can have the baby."

The court was an imposing building. We hurried up the steps and found the room we were assigned, then waited nervously outside on a bench for our 2 P.M. meeting with the judge. "What is said in court is confidential," said Julius. "You can go to jail for discussing what goes on outside the courtroom."

I could feel my heart begin to race, and then suddenly the door opened. A young couple came out, and the woman was weeping. I wanted to bolt out of the building and kidnap my baby.

Before I could, a young woman with spiky henna-red hair and a minidress appeared. "Hello," she said in English. "I will be your translator."

A second later we were ushered into the judge's chambers, a formal and austere room, with the judge's bench rising high above everybody else at one end. Three women, who looked kindly but as nervous as we did, filed in and stood at the side — a representative from the orphanage, one from the adoption council, and a social worker. We all stood, anxiously waiting for the judge. A moment later a handsome man in robes walked in solemnly, and proceedings for our destiny began. I was told by the translator to appear at the lectern to answer the first questions. As I stiffly walked to the podium I had the distinct impression I was being accused of a crime.

The judge grilled me. He asked whether I thought I was prepared to be a mother. He asked about our finances. He asked whether Willem was a good husband and whether he'd be a good father. He asked about my health. He asked whether I thought I was too old to be a mother. He asked why we had come to Lithuania. He asked if I knew what a big job it was to be a mother. He asked whether I could educate my child. He asked how I would work and care for a baby. Because of the tension and jet lag and the constant barrage of questions ricocheting from him to the translator to me, I felt woozy. The questioning and answering droned on until I thought I would faint, and then, mercifully, just when I thought I would fall down, he asked me to return to my chair.

Then the judge went to work on Willem. Question after question as if we were menaces to society. I tried to read the faces of the translator and of the three other women, but I saw nothing that gave a hint of how we were doing. At one point I glanced at my watch but realized I had put it on upside down. I tried to subtly pull my sleeve over my wrist so the judge wouldn't see that I couldn't even dress myself properly, let alone dress my baby. I thought I was dreaming when I heard the judge ask something, and the translator said, "It took you twenty years to find a wife and yet you want to be father to a baby you've only seen for one day?"

"I fell in love with my wife in one day as well," Willem said, and as the translator translated back into Lithuanian, the judge gave the slightest thread of a smile and I fell in love again with Willem.

But the judge continued on Willem, about our finances, his job, his moral character, on and on. And then, when I thought I was finally hallucinating, the judge asked a set of questions that sounded like they'd been dropped in by the writers on *Jeopardy*, including "Who wrote the Declaration of Independence?" and "What was the biggest challenge to the Dutch during the Middle Ages?"

After Willem deftly talked about Thomas Jefferson and the floods and the dikes, the judge rose, and we all stood up again, and the translator explained that the judge would leave the chambers for fifteen minutes to decide our case.

The judge swiftly walked out, we all sat down, and the Lithuanian women talked quietly with one another. Willem and I didn't say a word. Ten minutes passed and the judge returned. We all stood up again and he asked Willem and me to go to the lectern. There was a lot of talk in Lithuanian among the judge, the three women, and the translator. Finally, finally, when I thought I wouldn't be able to breathe, the translator turned to us and smiled and pronounced that we can be parents of our dear baby, if, *if*, she said, the birth parents do not change their minds over the next three and a half weeks. After that, and only after that, can we leave the country with our son. Until then we are allowed to visit him in the orphanage.

After we left the chambers, Julius leaped off the bench and shook our hands. "Congratulations," he said when he heard the news. "He's supposed to be one of the toughest judges in the country."

We all laughed nervously and said good-bye to the translator and the other women.

"I want to see our baby again," I announced.

"You have a whole lifetime," said Julius. "Aren't

you tired?" But when he saw the look in my eye he said, "No problem," and Willem did not object.

A few minutes later we collapsed into a rickety cab. The driver drove one block and suddenly stopped the car and began backing up very fast on a busy street, all the way back to the courthouse. "Broken." He shrugged as we got out and found another cab.

This time I had to control myself from running up the steps at the orphanage. We played with our son in the playroom for almost an hour. He's very alert and giggles a lot. He sits up and has a wonderfully sturdy little body. Several other babies crawled over to us, and I had the urge to take them all home.

I have the strong sense that for many years I've lived my life as if I was taking pictures with no film in the camera.

May 23, 1996

We have rented two rooms in an apartment complex on the outskirts of the city from a woman with four children, two of whom are out of the house. The building itself is falling apart, and the stairwells look like a slum. Postcommunism has created chaos, but the apartment itself is cozy. Although we have our own bathroom, we will share their kitchen. The mother is always out working. There's a sixteen-year-old girl, Maria, who speaks quite good English, and her blushing, red-headed, fifteen-year-old brother, Darius. She wants to be a lawyer, he wants to be an artist, and they both love the NBA and MTV. They've put a crib in our room for when we get our son.

Julius has gone to Warsaw and won't return until it's time for us to get our baby out of the orphanage. Then we'll go to the American embassy here for the baby's documents, then back to Warsaw for the baby's immigration visa. We are on our own now. I am used to knowing at least some of the language of a country when traveling but I'm at sea in Vilnius. The older people know a bit of German from the war, so Willem will have to steer us around. We went to the supermarket today, a cold, strangely quiet place with the minimum of goods, and we had to check our bags at the door, like Americans do in bookstores. We will be needing formula and baby food, but for now we have bread, cheese, and chocolate bars.

May 24, 1996

Today was a nightmare. Maria called a taxi for us, and we were very proud that with our dictionary and a map we could explain to the driver that we wanted to go to the orphanage. But when we arrived and eagerly entered the playroom, the nurse brought us our baby, saying he was very sick. He had a frightening cough and green fluid was coming out of his ears. Our jolly baby wouldn't stop crying. Using our Baltic phrase book and dictionary, we had a laborious conversation with the nurse, who said the baby needed attention immediately and would have to go to the hospital. The room spun, and I had to sit down on a tiny child's table. I asked for some juice, not realizing what a luxury that was, and after a very long time a kind woman brought me a glass of stuff that tasted like powdered fruit drink. I watched in a stupor as the baby was bundled in layer after layer until he looked like a sad, stuffed pierogi, and then a solemn woman appeared, who may have been a social worker, and said clearly and slowly in English, "Do not leave baby alone in hospital. Do not leave him alone there. Wait here for papers."

I wandered out into the hallway to catch my breath and out of the blue, two young men, who looked extraordinarily neat and extraordinarily American, bumped into me.

"Hi there," one said. "We're from Salt Lake City," and I realized they were Mormons.

"Hi there," I said, not eager to chat.

"Where are you from?" one asked.

"New York," I mumbled.

"Well, that's great. We were in JFK two weeks ago."

I fled back to my baby.

One hour passed and we were still at the orphanage waiting for the paperwork. Willem went downstairs to tell our taxi not to "palau" anymore. During that time I held the baby and rocked him and rocked him until he fell into a fitful sleep. We couldn't imagine why the paperwork was taking so long. Another hour passed. Finally the nurse brought in the baby's papers. The paperwork had not been done on a computer or even a typewriter.

It was all written beautifully in Lithuanian by hand, in ink. We had no idea what the papers said. And then, escorted by a nurse, we went in an orphanage car to a hospital a few minutes away.

The hospital is a stark, vast, stone building, not an inviting place. I held the baby as the nurse led us into a dark, cold hallway full of women holding their babies, all of whom were swaddled tightly with thick hats pulled down over their ears. Willem was the only man in sight. We waited for a long time in that hallway, as people stared at us. They could tell we were foreign, but I don't know if they knew we were American, or at least if I was American or not. I tried to look like I'd been holding my baby for seven months. Mothers and babies went in and out of a door, and after twenty-five minutes a woman in white appeared and motioned to us. Our nurse handed her our papers, spoke in rapid Lithuanian, then said good-bye to us. We sat in the examining room as this woman doctor examined the baby and he screamed, and then she painstakingly wrote up another report by hand in ink.

"Aciu, thank you," Willem and I kept saying "Aciu, Aciu," hoping that would help.

We were then led up several wide flights of steps and brought into a room with five empty cribs, one old sink, and dirty walls.

I did not want to put the baby down anywhere, but he had fallen into a feverish sleep, and he was very heavy. There was one crib that was slightly apart from the others, and I figured that if the room filled up, perhaps if he were a few inches away from the other babies that would save him. I put him down and he began crying again. Ten minutes later a nurse came in, nodded at us, pulled down some layers of the baby's clothing, and swiftly gave him an injection. He howled and I had the urge to climb in the crib with him, but soon he drifted off.

And then some kind of angel appeared, a lovely, dark-haired pediatrician in her thirties who could speak pretty good English. English was like candy to my ears. But she repeated what the social worker had said, about her own hospital. "Do not leave him alone here. I'm sorry for our facilities. We don't have the staff to take care of him. Can you afford a private nurse? He has pneumonia."

I could see Willem's head spinning.

"Yes," I blurted out. "Whatever is needed."

The pediatrician said, "I'll be back," and left abruptly.

Willem and I sat down on two square wooden stools and stared at our baby's beautiful, red, fevered face and his halting breath.

The pediatrician appeared ten minutes later. "Would four litas an hour be too much?" she said. That was one dollar.

For the first time that day, Willem and I smiled.

We spent the whole day in the hospital. Every couple of hours a nurse came in, put drops in his nose, ears, and mouth, and gave his bottom another shot. There is no hot water in the sink. There is no toilet paper in the bathroom. There are no diapers. In the orphanage they used worn pieces of cloth, no safety pins, but the babies were swaddled so tightly there was no need. They do have disposable syringes here. Everything else is reused. Willem went out for several hours and came back with a full backpack and tales of using his rusty German. "I talked with my hands and feet," he said as he proudly unpacked Pampers for 9-kilo babies, Similac with iron, and jars of Gerber baby food with Polish writing on the labels. Neither of us understands Polish, but there was a small picture of carrots and peas and the powdered Similac has many more vitamins than the watery formula he's been on for seven months. But so far he's not taking food or liquid.

That night we sang "Frère Jacques" to the baby, and then an older woman wearing a bathrobe came in, pointed to the baby, and smiled. At first I thought she was a patient who had wandered in from another floor, but then we realized she would be his private nurse for the night.

"Aciu, aciu," we said, and she pointed to the eight on her watch, and we understood she would be there until eight in the morning.

Willem put forty-eight litas on the windowsill, held down with a can of Similac. Twelve dollars for twelve hours' work.

May 25, 1996

The sun is out for the first time, and it's the first time I'm not shivering. The baby's fever is down two degrees, although he still is not eating and barely drinks his formula. The doctors are excellent and caring. The medicine is mostly old and Russian.

The pediatrician said, "The baby needs antibiotics and he should have better ones than we can give him." She handed Willem a prescription for a German drug on a tiny, rough piece of paper. When he asked what drugstore would have it, she only shrugged. Willem looked exhausted but kissed me and the baby, then took his map and backpack and went out on one of his hunting-and-gathering missions. I stayed with the baby, playing the tapes I'd brought on our small tape recorder, featuring "The Wheels on the Bus" and "John Jacob Jingleheimer Schmidt."

It began to rain again, and there was no heat in the hospital room. I covered the baby as well as I could with a stained comforter. He lay on a big pillow with his beautiful eyes closed, and I prayed. That was all I figured I could do, that and sing my repertoire of children's songs, which is limited to "Frère Jacques" and "The Wheels on the Bus." Willem was gone so long I became worried and had the dark thought of being a widow in this country, not knowing the language, with a seriously ill baby in the hospital, a baby who of course still might not be ours. I prayed the baby would eat and prayed he would not die, and I prayed he could be our son and I thought of the little baby girl we never got and wondered if she died alone in this hospital. Willem finally returned after over two hours, with wet shoes and chilled hands, but also with a damp bag of the precious German antibiotics. An hour later the pediatrician appeared and he handed the bag to her like it was the Golden Fleece. She simply said, "Good," but she seemed impressed. I think Willem has passed a major test.

There have been more scandals, or at least rumors of more scandals, about foreign adoptions here, babies abused, babies abandoned. They hear about babies being thrown out of windows in New York City, and some people feel Americans are monsters. We are the only foreigners at this hospital, the only people trying to adopt a baby. Today five people, I don't even know who they were — hospital staff? patients? visitors? — just walked into our room, looked at us, looked at our baby, nodded, and left.

Last night we returned to the apartment and young Darius knocked on our door as we sat exhausted on the bed, trying to make ourselves eat heavy black bread, even though neither of us had an appetite.

"Yes?" I said weakly. "Yes?"

"Would you like to see my book on bonsai?" he asked.

"Bonsai?" I said.

"Yes, little trees."

"Yes, I know. Yes, I would." I smiled. As difficult a situation as we're in, I love this country. I waited at the door for Darius, and he came back a few minutes later with a big coffee table book, in English and Lithuanian, on bonsai.

I cannot imagine ever having the energy to read any book again, on bonsai or anything else.

"Thank you," I said to Darius as he handed me the book.

"Good night," he said. "May you be dreaming sweet."

May 26, 1996

In the hospital a cart comes around three times a day with kasha, "the kasha wagon," we call it, and a woman with massive arms sets out a big metal plate for the baby. Today, for the first time, the baby took a few bites, but we have not yet attempted the Gerber baby food. He took a few sips of tea, which was very sweet, although he has not gone back to either the hospital formula or the Similac. The nurses keep pointing to his eyelashes and mine, to say we look alike. I sang "The Wheels on the Bus" infinite times, adding my own verses. My personal favorites are "The pizza on the bus goes cheese, cheese, cheese" and "the wallpaper is busy, busy, busy."

May 27, 1996

Rejoice, rejoice, the baby is eating the kasha, and I gave him a jar of baby food carrots and peas, which he gobbled up, and he's beginning to take the Similac. I wanted to hug the pediatrician. She says he will be in the hospital for a week, and then he is legally supposed to return to the orphanage, but we don't want him going back there. We don't want to leave him again, we don't want him to be around other children who might be sick, and we want to be able to give him Similac and our baby food. I don't know how we'll swing it, but I'm not going to let him go back.

Today was a beautiful spring day, and instead of returning to the apartment, Willem insisted we go into the city. He trekked me through the old section with its medieval towers, where children with long braids and boys with breeches were folk dancing in the street. And we went into a wonderfully ornate Russian Orthodox cathedral and stopped to eat blinis sold by a woman with a cart. Now that my son is eating I feel I can eat as well. Then we went for bitter strong coffee in a café, and Bon Jovi was playing on MTV, but I could not get "The Wheels on the Bus" out of my head.

May 28, 1996

Maria knocked on the door this morning and said she had made us breakfast. We did not pay for food when we rented the room, but she insisted. We ate sausage and potatoes and delicious, hearty soup while we watched Michael Jackson on MTV.

May 29, 1996

The pediatrician has set up a wonderful team of women to care for the baby—a pediatric resident, a nurse who wears red patent leather shoes, and the grandmother, Mrs. T., who wore a bathrobe when we first met her. I had a fleeting fear that my son will never think of me as his mother, because he's been cared for by so many different women, but I had no time to dwell on this thought. Today, when we arrived, I panicked because our son was not in his room. After a frantic search, we found him in another wing. It turns out there's a virus going around and two babies have died, so he was moved. When we found him, he had on a pink bonnet with big puffs of cotton in his ears. He looks like an aviator. Miraculously, his fever is gone. We wheeled him around in a newborn cart to celebrate, which made him smile.

Last night I could not sleep. I kept wondering where the baby's birth mother is. Did I see her in the supermarket? Was she checking her bag at the counter next to me? Did she drive by in a car? Did our shoulders brush on one of the narrow streets in the old city? Will she want her sweet son back? Sometimes Willem and I call him by his Lithuanian name and sometimes by the name we've chosen for him, and often we call him Kuba, the Polish nickname for his English name, prounounced "Coobah," given to him by Mrs. T.

May 30, 1996

Today we left the hospital for two hours and went to two Catholic churches and one of the Jewish museums. The museum was practically bare, with a few relics from centuries gone by. There was a seventeenth-century wooden ark carved with animals and birds. The guide, who was a playwright and said her dream was to move to New York, said the ark had to do with the biblical passage that tells of the virtues of being strong like a lion, swift like a deer, fierce like a tiger, and able to fly like an eagle. I wanted to tell the guide that this is what I wished for our baby son who was in the hospital, but when she asked what we were doing in Lithuania we said we were tourists.

When we returned to the hospital, Mrs. T., in her bathrobe, insisted we get another hat for Kuba because the pink one is getting tight, so at the end of the day we went to a department store in the center of the city. There were no escalators or elevators, just a series of steep, dingy steps, and floors with a limited number of items, and as in the supermarket, it was eerily quiet. We found a simple green hat, and the clerk used an abacus to tally the three-dollar purchase. I am struck by the quietness of Lithuanians in public. Were they always like this? Was it because of World War II? The Russians? Our guidebook says there isn't one family who has not known someone who was either shot or sent to Siberia.

May 31, 1996

Is this Memorial Day? I feel so out of touch with America. Today I held Kuba in my arms at the hospital and read *Pat the Bunny* to him, and he stroked the bunny before he began gnawing on the book. Several people came in and looked at the book. They had never seen anything like it. All my life, from my childhood recollections of this classic, I thought that Pat was the name of the bunny, since it was my name as well. I had the revelation that "Pat" was a verb when Willem was out hunting down baby food, but I could not communicate my discovery to the nurse. Each day Willem has gone to different stores, because baby food is not always available each day at the same place, so it's been a treasure hunt. There are few men in the hospital, few men visitors, and few men doctors. There are three little girls, big girls compared to our son, five- and six-year-olds, in the room next door to him, Natasha, Christina, and Julia, also from the Children's House, which is what they call the orphanage in English. They love to push Kuba around in the newborn cart and keep lifting up their arms for Willem to give them rides on his shoulders. I love to see Willem surrounded by all these children.

June 1, 1996

Last night we watched CNN before we fell asleep. It was beautiful watching the weather commentator talk of storm systems across Lithuania, Latvia, and Belarus. Eastern Europe feels very foreign and very familiar to me. I've been waiting to see that weather map for a very long time.

June 2, 1996

I feel desperate to get Kuba out of the hospital. As well as he's being treated there, I want him away from all that illness. This morning we were instructed to take him for a massage. We bundled him in a down comforter and carried him through the cold, dank hallways to the masseuse. She was an enormous woman who rubbed him vigorously. At first he giggled, but then he turned so red I wanted to steal him from her arms, but we have to play by the rules here. As anxious as I am to get him out of the hospital, I'm not ready to leave Lithuania yet. I like our little world here. I feel so close to Willem, and we keep meeting such wonderful people. Today we had lunch in the small dining room at the hospital. We were the only Americans and the only non-Lithuanians there. There were a few people wearing bathrobes and I finally realized that the visitors and nurses are the ones who wear bathrobes here, not the patients. A delightful woman behind the counter patiently helped us with the menu, and we ended up with delicious borscht with potato and some kind of wonderful pastries. The pediatrician said the whole hospital knows we're trying to adopt this baby.

This afternoon, while Kuba slept, Willem insisted we go to the Holocaust Museum, a green wooden building that looked innocent enough on the outside but inside was full of exhibits on the horror of the extraordinarily quick obliteration of Jewish life. We were the only ones there. Then we took a walk to Vilnius University, a four-hundred-year-old school full of spectacular archways and courtyards. If it weren't for Willem, I wouldn't see one thing here. I'd take care of the baby and sleep. This evening when we returned from the hospital I was exhausted, but Willem was bursting with energy. He went to play basketball at a sports center with Darius and returned sweaty and happy. At the entrance to the gymnasium he said a nurse inspected everybody's hands and feet.

June 3, 1996

Last night we had dinner at an outdoor café: an omelette, beet and herring salad, and borscht. It is summer weather now, and the women are suddenly wearing incredibly sexy clothes — tight jeans and T-shirts and high, high heels. My attire would best be described as rumpled. There was that twinkling evening light of northern Europe, and I thought of Kuba with cotton in his ears and his little green hat, never being outside except for the ride from the orphanage to the hospital, and I thought of those little girls running through the hallways and I wanted to go prop a ladder up against the window of the hospital and help them all escape. When we got back to the apartment Maria and Darius were watching *General Hospital* on TV.

When we arrived at the real hospital this morning we were told Kuba had to have an X ray to check his lungs before he could be discharged. I could see that he is much better and didn't want him to have it, but I had to be patient and do as they say. Willem carried Kuba, while Mrs. T. in her bathrobe and I followed them down the corridor to the X-ray room. I gasped when I saw the equipment. The room was strung with crisscrossed wires as if there had been a terrible storm and all the power lines blew down. The equipment had the look of old Russian artillery. The X-ray technician, a rotund woman in a leather apron, kept pointing to Willem, and first we thought she was telling him to leave. We finally realized he was being asked to participate in the ordeal.

Kuba was strapped tightly to a board, with his arms and legs buckled down. Then he was blindfolded. The screaming he let out chilled my bones. Then the X-ray woman strapped a leather apron on Willem. I was sure both my husband and baby would die. The X-ray woman shooed the nurse and me out of the room, and as we were leaving I could see Willem holding the baby up in front of him in a strange hanging contraption with chains. Mrs. T. and I, neither knowing the other's language, held each other's hands as we heard Kuba's piercing screams through the door. An eternity later it was over, and we could return to the room, unstrap our exhausted baby, and the procedure was over.

※　　※　　※

I pray that we get him out of the hospital and into the fresh air soon. Before we left the hospital this evening we were told by the pediatrician that he's been exposed to chicken pox, which is fine, but if he has visible spots, he won't be allowed to fly into the United States.

June 4, 1996 4 A.M.

I can't sleep. The Great Escape. Today is Father's Day in Lithuania, and Kuba is scheduled to be released from the hospital. The awful X-ray showed that his lungs are clear. Our new task is to convince the orphanage that we are fit enough parents to care for him on our own. We have been told to be at the hospital at nine o'clock, at which time papers will be drawn up (we know what that means), and someone from the orphanage will escort us back to the orphanage. When we're there, more papers will be written up, and, I hope, we will be able to leave. We've learned a few more words in Lithuanian. "One, two, three, yes, no," but not anything to convey our parenting skills.

After an exhausting night, we arrived at the hospital at nine, with the stroller, to find Kuba sitting up in his crib, playing with Mrs. T.'s bracelet. Mrs. T. sat on the wood stool next to him. I wanted to cry. I probably will never see this woman again, and she helped save my baby's life. "Aciu, aciu," we said over and over to her. We hugged, and she kissed Kuba, and when she left, I felt alone. We were about to leave the cocoon. But, of course, there were papers to be written.

"Palau, palau, wait, wait," we were told, and we waited three long hours with Kuba as the doctor and nurses wrote up careful notes on his case. As usual we had no idea what they said. A young, cheerful woman, who looked vaguely familiar, arrived with a bag of Lithuanian baby clothes, but I could not place her. She was very animated, and kept pointing first to Kuba and then to the clothes, but I could not understand what she was saying. Finally it dawned on me that she was from the orphanage and that we were supposed to put Kuba back in his orphanage togs.

The woman and I both started laughing because

it had taken so long to communicate, but I showed her the little blue-and-white striped overalls and T-shirt I'd brought with us, and she nodded and helped me dress the baby in those.

Afterward we bid a teary good-bye to the pediatrician and her staff, and took a picture of them with Kuba. The pediatrician said, "Maybe the baby will come back and be a doctor here some day."

I felt overwhelmed, excited to be a mother, scared to be a mother, and hoping I could start being a real mother today. The orphanage was only a ten-minute walk, but a taxi had been called for and it was not our place to object. In fact, Kuba smiled the whole way in the car, or "mašina" as it's called in Lithuania.

When we arrived back at the orphanage, Willem and Kuba and I grew very quiet. It felt as if we'd been away a lifetime. As we climbed the steps to the playroom and sleeping room, I held Kuba tight. I was frightened we would have to leave him there. There were two babies in the playpen. When the nurse saw our baby she said, "Laba diena," and then she called him by his Lithuanian name. She went over to a cupboard and handed me a small pacifier. In fact, Kuba had refused a pacifier whenever we offered it to him in the hospital. I wanted to say "No, no, take that away," but she kept saying the baby's Lithuanian name and I understood that it was his. I said, "Aciu, thank you," as graciously as I could, but I put it in my pocket. Then, as Willem went off with the woman who escorted us from the hospital to see what he could do about our papers, the nurse pulled me gently by the arm into the sleeping room with the six cribs. She kept pointing to the crib our baby had slept in and I realized she was saying it was time for a morning nap, but I held Kuba close. "No, thank you. Aciu, aciu," I said over and over.

An hour passed, with me walking around, trying to entertain Kuba and be friendly to the babies in the playpen at the same time. The only moment there was real communication between the nurse and me was when she pointed to Kuba's strong legs and said "NBA, NBA," and we both smiled.

And then Willem returned, followed by the director of the orphanage and the social worker who had warned us not to leave the baby alone in the hospital. They smiled, but I could not read their faces. I tried to look as motherly as possible, and suddenly I blurted out, "We'll take good care of him. We'll give him the best care," as I stroked my son's hair.

Willem said quietly to me, "It's okay. Let's go. We can leave."

I looked at him questioningly and felt a wave of excitement as I understood that he meant with the baby, with our baby, that is. We shook hands with the director of the orphanage and the social worker. We said good-bye to the nurse and she and I patted Kuba's legs and we both said "NBA" at the same time.

When Willem and I got downstairs we put Kuba in the stroller and struggled with the safety straps for the first time. We each took a handle and rolled him gently down the driveway from the orphanage, and by the time we reached the front gate, he was sound asleep. At this pivotal moment in his young life, he was snoozing.

"Aciu," I said to Willem. "What did you tell them?"

"I told them that we would take good care of him and had everything set up for him back at the apartment, and as soon as we got back to America we would take him to the pediatrician."

"Aciu," I said, reaching up to kiss him, and then

the stroller jammed. I bent down and examined the wheels. A pinecone had gotten stuck. I removed it and put it in my pocket.

"A pineapple?" said Willem.

He's always called pinecones "pineapples" and I've never corrected him, and I did not then either.

We strolled Kuba down the sunny street, past a bus depot, and we stopped to take a picture of him and the buses.

"Do you have any kids?" I asked Willem.

"Yes," he said. "I have a son."

In the taxi the driver made no sign that he thought this baby was not our child. When he dropped us off he held up two fists in the air and said, "Strong baby."

Maria and Darius were home from school, back at the apartment, and they hugged and kissed us and the baby. Then we all sat on the couch and watched a Lithuanian quiz show.

Last night we were exhausted. Kuba cried and cried when we first put him in his little crib at eight thirty, but we played the music tapes over and over

and then sang "Frère Jacques" and finally he fell
sound asleep.

June 6, 1996

Baby's Schedule
6:35 A.M. Warm bottle of Similac with iron
8:15–9:00 Sleep

(Darius came by at eight thirty this morning with
prosciutto and cucumber sandwiches, orange juice
and ice cream. I think he thinks Americans eat ice
cream all the time. The three of us sat silently and
ate as the baby slept.)

10:45 Jar of Gerber chicken and peas (We think
   it's chicken; the picture looks like a rooster, but
   babies probably don't eat roosters.)
1:45 P.M. Similac and zwieback
2:45–3:45 Sleep
4:45 Bottle
6:00 Gerber banana baby food

9:00 Sleep

9:20 Willem and I went to bed

June 7, 1996

It was a spring day, and we took Kuba out for a walk in the world. He has a delightfully sunny "character," as my grandmother would say. We wheeled him along the cobblestones in the old city and he reached out his little arms at a balloon, dogs, the trolley, the breeze . . . People stared at us. Could they tell we're new parents, that our baby is Lithuanian? It could also be because of our stroller, which looks like a Rolls-Royce compared to the rusty ones here.

We are taking lots of pictures to make an album for the baby when he is older. I have visions of him bringing it to school for Show-and-Tell.

We passed a woman next to a large stand-up scale, and realized that if we paid her a few cents, we could be weighed. Willem and Kuba had no interest, but I couldn't pass up the opportunity. I paid the woman and hopped on the scale. She adjusted the weights and held up four fingers.

"Four?" I said. "I weigh four?" but that's as much as I could figure out, which made no sense in either kilograms or pounds.

Willem made fun of me in Dutch to Kuba and I made fun of myself in English and Kuba gave us both the most quizzical look. I think he misses the Lithuanian language.

June 8, 1996

I feel fragile, as if I've just brought my new baby home from the hospital, which in fact I have, but Willem wants us to take him sightseeing. I'm not so eager. I just want to keep him healthy until we leave, and I'm nervous his birth parents will see him and take him back. Willem has none of these fears. He's intent on seeing every single monument in the guidebook and even wants to go to a concert. His boundless energy continues to be a godsend when it comes to supplies for the baby. Each day he returns from the supermarket with a stash of food and formula and household goods, all of which take a certain amount of effort to track down.

I don't want to stop Willem from his exploring,

but I don't have the energy to go with him, and so I've encouraged him to go on his own. Taking care of Kuba is enough of a new world for me right now. And when I need help, Maria has been wonderful. School is out for summer vacation and she's made savory blintzes and is a natural with babies. She looks more like Kuba does than I do, which occasionally makes me sad, but those moments pass quite quickly.

June 9, 1996

Kuba had his first black-market banana today and it was a hit. I fed him as I watched CNN, all about an Australian woman who is swimming from Florida to Cuba in a shark cage, while Willem went to a Holocaust memorial on the outskirts of town. At five this morning Darius and his mother left for a holiday in Italy. At midnight last night we had a party with almond cake and sugary cookies and they gave us three presents—lyrical wind chimes, an embroidered lace doily, and a picture inlaid with amber stones, all typically Lithuanian. Willem danced with Kuba on his shoulders. Then Darius solemnly presented me with an intricate painting he had made of American Indians and teepees.

I don't want to go home. I love when Willem comes back from his adventures full of news and a backpack of food. We gave Kuba his first official bath in the sink today. He loved the water, but as we washed him, I could see a cloud fall over Willem's face in the mirror. I knew what it was. His mother had given him cold showers in Holland when he was a boy.

"I would have given you warm baths when you were a little boy," I said, but then Kuba started to wiggle out of our hands and we had to catch him. When I was a little girl I was fascinated by the book *Ripley's Believe It or Not.* My all-time favorite entry was about a newborn baby boy in Russia, who could stand up in his father's palm. This baby is like that. He's very much the circus baby I dreamed of months ago.

June 10, 1996

I'm so tired I feel sick. My arms feel like they're going to fall off. Suddenly carrying nineteen pounds has taken its toll. I can't tell how much has to do with the trip and adoption or just being a plain old mother. Old feels like the operative word. I had to put on my glasses, my bifocals(!), to cut the baby's fingernails. "That's your problem" is one of the few English expressions I've heard here, and this is my problem.

Today, while Willem visited the site where the Lithuanians fought for independence from Russia five years ago, I lay on the floor next to Kuba as he slept on a blanket. He is breathing so evenly now. As I stared at his exquisite face I noticed fine blue veins at his temples, and for a moment I could imagine him as an old man dying. When will that be? I hope he lives to be a very old man, but I will miss that. Will he miss me?

I picked up one of the guidebooks Willem had left behind. I read that the stork is the national bird, which seems fitting, but my eyes were too lazy to read more, so I turned on the television quietly to a Lithuanian music show, where a trombone player was saying in broken English "I love Sammy Dave. Sammy Dave, he is my favorite."

June 11, 1996

Praise the Lord. The appeal period is over. Julius called this morning. He is back in Vilnius, and even though he was only a few miles away, the connection was terrible. We could barely hear him, and he could not hear us, but we figured out that we were supposed to meet him at one of the government offices. When we arrived at 10 A.M. and stood out on the sidewalk, we greeted one another like family and he gave the baby a big hug. He had heard from the orphanage about our time at the hospital. There have been many, many conversations, some in our presence and some privately—in Lithuanian and Polish—that we have missed entirely.

The government office was not actually open the hours that were posted on the door, so for the next three hours we took a walk with Kuba, taking turns carrying him, because we had not brought the stroller. We made one stop for blinis, and Julius talked to Kuba in Polish, Willem spoke Dutch, and I cooed in English. When we returned to the office, we waited in a long line of frustrated people. "Palau, palau." It felt like we were at the Motor Vehicles Department, and in fact I'm not exactly sure where we were. The only person who seemed to enjoy being there was a woman who looked like she was wearing a Cat in the Hat costume and tickled Kuba's toes.

We legally have a baby now. I am legally a mother. Our next step before we can leave Lithuania will be the American embassy. When we returned to the apartment, Willem and I sat Kuba between us on the couch, and I read *Pat the Bunny* aloud. It seemed the best way to celebrate, but when I turned to the page with the tiny mirror in the book, I could see tears in my eyes.

June 12, 1996

Yesterday, while Willem was out delivering some of our documents to Julius, Maria came over and watched Kuba for twenty minutes so I could go to the store. Walking alone in the bright Baltic sunshine I felt a burst of elation that I was finally a mother and also incredibly light, walking just on my own. Everything seems to be set in vivid relief.

This morning we went with Julius to the American embassy, which was like going to the moon. The building and grounds were startlingly new and clean and bright, with the red, white, and blue flag snapping smartly in the breeze outside like a commercial. We set Kuba down on the counter at the security check and he charmed the guards. Then we walked with him through the metal detectors into this American haven.

We were the only ones in the sparkling waiting room.

"What's up?" a clean-shaven young man in khakis said at the counter.

We handed him all our precious papers, and he took them away. In less then ten minutes he returned with a small folded piece of paper that says "Children's Travel Document," with a little photo glued in that Julius had given us. In it Kuba is wearing a sweater with hearts on it that must have been donated to the orphanage, but this document now has his American name. Along with the passport was a small stack of papers, half in Lithuanian, half carefully translated in English, all tied with beautiful purple string like a special gift.

And then we were off to have more photographs

of the baby taken for the immigration papers we will get in Poland. For all official documents, the right ear must be visible. Trying to explain the importance of turning the right ear to the camera to a seven-month-old was a slapstick affair.

In two hours we will leave for the airport to fly to Warsaw. In two hours our baby will leave his homeland. Kuba is cheerful and keeps pulling off his socks, but Willem and I are sad to leave. It's been challenging, but our mission has been clear. We've knit together a little family here. There's been no phone ringing, no answering machine to rule our days. There's been the excitement of being surrounded by a foreign language, and I will miss everybody who helped us become parents.

June 13, 1996

The Vilnius Airport was nothing like I remembered it; the departures area was very modern. We set Kuba on the floor, and he was in heaven, gazing up at huge model airplanes hanging from the ceiling. Willem wandered off at one point, and I figured he'd found one last place to explore, but he came back with a pair of amber earrings from the gift shop.

"Aciu," I said. "Aciu, aciu" when he presented them to me.

We all sat on the floor and I put on the earrings and Kuba tried to pull them off.

Then they were calling our flight, and it appeared that there was only a handful of other people headed for Warsaw. We awkwardly folded the stroller and struggled with our bags, and carried Kuba to the gate. When we handed over Willem's Dutch passport, my American passport, and the baby's little Lithuanian travel document, many eyebrows were raised, and for fifteen minutes there was a heated discussion among several people in uniforms. They did not look pleased, but finally they waved us through. As we walked outside, there was a burst of wind, and I covered Kuba's ears with my hands. I felt like I'd just won a giant capture-the-flag game.

For over a year I've been worried about flying with the baby. I even asked the pediatrician in New

York before we left if the cabin pressure could hurt his little ears.

"Be sure to have him suck on something or drink on takeoff and landing," he said.

Our baby had no interest; he's given up pacifiers for life and pushed away the bottle when I held it to his lips. As Lithuania lay below us in great swatches of emerald green and we flew west to Poland, I dramatically said, "Good-bye, Lietuva, good-bye," but Kuba had become fascinated with the buckle of the seat belt.

June 14, 1996

When we got off the plane last night, Julius was there, appearing like a magician. He helped us with our bags and took us straight to the pediatrician, who had to give the baby a clean bill of health before he would be allowed to enter the United States. The doctor beamed when she saw him. "He'll be walking in a month," she said as he yanked the stethoscope off her ears.

Warsaw feels like Paris after Vilnius. The hotel we're staying in is Shangri-la, with room service and hot water and even a minibar. Of course Willem could not resist seeing "some of Warsaw when we're here," and of course the baby was enough of a new country for me.

Yesterday afternoon, though, he kept crying and I lay with him on the bed, stroking his head. That didn't work, so I looked him in the eye and whispered, "Why are you crying? We're not leaving you here. We're all going together to America. Did I ever tell you the story of the mermaid and the elephant?" His crying began to subside. "Once upon a time there was a mermaid and an elephant who were very much in love. (I often called Willem an elephant because he has a loud sneeze.) They wanted a baby very much and one day they were walking in the forest and came upon a beautiful baby tiger. They fell in love with him instantly and said, 'Will you be our baby?'

"The tiger said, 'But you don't know what food I like or what games I like to play.'

"We'll learn,' we promised. . . ."

Miraculously, at this point, either out of boredom or fatigue, Kuba fell asleep in my arms.

Breakfast was included at our fancy hotel, so this morning we played with Kuba from six A.M. until eight when the restaurant opened. Tickling him is like playing a lovely instrument.

After a buffet, where we stuffed ourselves with melon and cheesecake and eggs, Julius met us in the lobby and we walked against a strong wind the three blocks to the American embassy. An enormous line snaked around the block, but because we had an infant, we were ushered through quite quickly. Once inside, however, we entered a large, chilly waiting room jammed with people. There was not a single empty seat so we perched Kuba on a counter, while Julius went to get us the proper forms. We had to fill out two, one for immigration into the United States and one for adoption.

We tried to keep Kuba occupied, but it was impossible to write and hold him at the same time, so Julius kindly entertained him while we dealt with the forms.

The adoption form was fairly standard, except it did ask "Does the child have trouble with parental authority?" I asked this to Kuba directly, at which point he waved his hands around, and all our papers scattered to the floor.

The immigration form included such questions as "Do you plan to practice polygamy?"

We waited a total of two and a half hours at the embassy, mainly waiting for our papers "to be processed." I'm becoming a pro at changing the baby in public places. He remained jolly and even made friends with one little deaf boy who kept coming over and holding up his helicopter to show him. The room was full of a nervous buzz, some people going to visit relatives for the summer, others starting a new life in America. Most of them were Polish. I could see no other American-Dutch couples there with Baltic babes.

Last night, with the hotel room littered with Pampers and our precious envelopes of documents, Willem and I lay on the bed in a trance with Kuba between us, watching some kind of *Dating Game* in Polish. Willem and I ate salami sandwiches we had ordered from room service while Kuba gnawed on a zwieback.

June 15, 1996

We are in the Warsaw airport again. It is noon. Our plane is scheduled to leave at 1 P.M., for New

York, but there has been a delay. "Technical difficulties," we are told.

2 P.M.

Another delay. Technical difficulties. We've been wheeling Kuba around in the luggage cart. He seems to be the only person who is not cranky. The airport is the biggest, most bustling space he's ever been in, full of sounds and lights. We've been given a free lunch by LOT Polish Airlines.

4 P.M.

Technical difficulties. Nobody will tell us if or when our plane will be leaving.

8 P.M.

We've been told our plane will depart at 10 P.M., nine hours late. We just had another meal on the house, while Kuba took a nap in the luggage cart.

We have used up all our formula and are down to one diaper.

June 16, 1996

The plane actually took off last night around ten thirty, and we got a free seat between us for the baby. I was able to scrunch down next to him, and after stroking his cheek and singing to him, he fell asleep, and slept until just before we landed in New York. Willem and I did not sleep a wink.

Today is Father's Day in America, and we landed at Kennedy Airport at 3 A.M. The airport was hot and humid in that special New York summer way. When we arrived at Customs, the line was short, one of the benefits of a 3 A.M. arrival, and the Customs agent did not bat an eye at our three different passports. We were then directed to go to a special room marked IMMIGRATION. This was the Ellis Island of the end of the twentieth century, a small room full of sad, exhausted grownups. We had the only baby immigrant. I carried Kuba, who was now wide awake and ready for action, to the front desk. A woman in uniform looked up from her papers, and I said, as graciously as I could, "Our plane was nine hours late, I'm out of formula, and we just adopted this baby," all of which were "true facts," as I used to say as a child.

The immigration officer smiled at Kuba and said she would see what she could do. Five minutes later another woman in uniform appeared and asked for our papers. We handed them to her, she gave them a quick look, and nodded.

Kuba started waving both arms up and down in a gleeful greeting as if he were conducting a small orchestra, and she said, "He's won me over. Welcome to America, baby."

June 21, 1996

I'm so exhausted I feel bruised. Kuba has immediately found a schedule of going to bed at 8 P.M. and awaking at exactly 6 in the morning like a little rooster, but as ragged as I am, I barely sleep. When we arrived home there was an enormous card taped to our front door, welcoming the baby and signed by everybody in our building. People I hardly know ring the doorbell with good wishes and gifts. There was advice from Laura on the answering machine. "Be sure to answer the door in your bathrobe so folks will get the message that you might be just a wee bit tired." I think there is more attention because our son is adopted, but I have no way to judge. I did read somewhere, long ago, when I had time to read, that people feel adopted children belong to the world.

June 22, 1996

When I bent down to get the New York *Times* at the front door the other day (which day I'm not entirely sure; the days of the week have melted into one another), there was a front-page article on children from Russia, adopted by Americans, who have turned out to be pyromaniacs.

Today, when a neighbor came by to meet the baby, she studied Kuba sucking on a rubber ball on the kitchen floor and pronounced, "He looks okay. Do you know anything about his parents?"

I was tempted to say, "We're terrific, don't you think?" and light a match, but refrained.

June 23, 1996

My parents and grandmother came to meet Kuba. I was in awe watching my almost-nine-month-old baby from Lithuania and his great-grandmother, whose mother came from Poland, sitting on the couch together, eating grapes. My grandmother is 1,104 months old.

June 24, 1996

Willem has gone back to work full time, and I am alone in the city, in the summer. As spanking-new baby presents arrive daily for Kuba, I frantically rummage around for a rattle I made from an old aspirin container with Lithuanian pennies in it. Teaching won't start until the fall, but I'm concerned I'll be eternally askew, that I'll permanently have dried formula on my shoulder. Now that tracking down food, formula, and Pampers is not such an adventure, they do not have quite the allure they used to. I'm deeply in love with my son, but I'm certain the days are doubly as long as they used to be.

June 25, 1996

When I was a little girl I was always frightened to run into the jump rope when two other girls swung it around. I feel the same way now, but I have no choice but to enter into the chaotic kingdom of the playground.

Today, after Willem left for work and Kuba had already been doing extensive research in the apartment for three hours, I planned my debut. It was easy to dress Kuba in his sweet sun suit and tiny plastic jelly sandals, but what about my playground couture? I've never felt comfortable in shorts. Nobody informed me twenty years ago that I might as well feel comfortable with my body at twenty-two, because it doesn't get any better at forty-two. As Kuba chewed on the shoes on the floor of my closet, I finally settled on my old khaki pants and white T-shirt uniform, sneakers, and my hair in a pony tail.

I entered the playground pushing Kuba ahead of me as a shield, trying to create an aura of someone who'd been doing this for eight months already, my son and I, I and my son, both of us pros at the American sandbox scene.

But in the buzz of activity our arrival did not cause a stir. At this moment, as I surveyed the crowded jungle gyms and slides, sprinklers and swings, I knew I'd joined the great anonymous mass of motherhood. I quickly pushed Kuba toward a bench, unbuckled him, and carried him to the sandbox.

A perky young mother who was wise enough to be proud of her body in her twenties said, "What a cute baby! Have I seen you before? Was he born at Roosevelt Hospital?"

Was this woman some kind of a spy?

"No, no," I said. "He was born out of the city," and I began furiously digging a hole in the sand with my fingers. Just what am I supposed to tell people about my son?

I said hello to eight women today: three mothers and five baby-sitters, from Guyana, Paraguay, Guadalupe, Ireland, and the Bronx. I soon learned that the polite greeting is "How old is your child?" and that names are given out much later. I felt more comfortable with the baby-sitters. I'm not sure if it's because I'd just come from a foreign country or because my son is from a foreign country, or because I feel I'm on foreign ground now. In the sandbox confessional I heard of one husband who was having an affair with his niece, a woman who had seven miscarriages, another who insisted that babies were toilet-trained by the age of one in her country, and a recipe for cardamom tea to get babies to sleep.

June 28, 1996

Yesterday was Willem's forty-sixth birthday. Other years I always baked him a cake, but as I staggered around with Kuba on my hip, "If You're Happy and You Know It" beating in my head, all I could manage was to scoop out ice cream and place a candle in it for dessert. After dinner, with Kuba reaching for the ice cream, I tried to light the candle, but, as Willem kindly pointed out, I had put it in upside down.

June 29, 1996

I took Kuba for a complete checkup today. The office was so modern and sparkling clean; it reminded me of the American embassy in Vilnius. I gave the doctor Kuba's medical papers from Lithuania, but he suggested he have all his blood tests done over again, including one for HIV. I felt annoyed and defensive about Eastern Europe, but I did not object. The examination went smoothly, and then a nurse came in and took a lot of Kuba's blood and gave him two injections, which did not please him at all. So far he had been immunized only for tuberculosis, so he has some shots to catch up on. He is now twenty-eight inches. I am sixty inches. My almost-nine-month-old son is almost half my height.

June 30, 1996

Today I took Kuba in the stroller and waited for Willem at the top of the subway steps when he came home from work. Six years ago I stood at the same spot waiting for him for a romantic rendez-vous with nothing on but a raincoat. Perhaps one day I'll stand in the same spot with a cane.

I miss Willem. I miss being a family in Lithuania. Since we've returned we've scattered apart like loose jacks thrown on the sidewalk.

July 1, 1996

While Kuba naps I turn on the television in a stu-por and am startled by all the movies and talk shows about reuniting children with their birth parents and weeping parents searching for their biological children. Each time I see one I frantically switch the channel. I don't want to be part of this subculture, but I am whether I like it or not.

July 2, 1996

When I was strolling Kuba through the park yesterday I saw a sign for NEW MOTHER'S GROUP. TUESDAY MORNINGS 10 A.M. AT THE HIPPOS. BRING YOUR OWN COFFEE. The hippos are lifelike sculptures with water spraying from their mouths in a playground in Riverside Park. Tomorrow I'll go. I imagine most of these mothers gave birth to their babies and are probably half my age. Plus, I can't imagine holding a hot cup of coffee with Kuba wriggling in my arms, but if I don't go, there's more than a slim possibility I'll go mad.

July 3, 1996

I went to the New Mother's Group, and not one of the twelve women had coffee in her hands. Indeed, most of them appeared to be ten years younger than I am and some were wearing shorter shorts than I ever felt comfortable in, but there were newborns to one-year-olds crawling and climbing over one another on a huge blanket, and Kuba immediately made his way into the center of the writhing crowd.

And then, I could not help myself, I began talking about the adoption, and the orphanage, and Lithuania, and blintzes . . . as if I had taken some kind of truth serum. I could not control myself. I don't know how long I babbled, but I sensed it was too long.

Someone said, "Where *is* Lithuania anyway?" and I began an Eastern Bloc geography lesson, saying that Lithuania, Latvia, and Estonia are as distinct as Mexico, the U.S., and Canada. Finally I shut up, when I heard another woman say "I just saw a documentary about Romania or somewhere . . . I'm not sure. It was awful . . ."

I felt that they were studying Kuba, looking for some deviant traits.

One woman said, "Weren't you scared just to take *any* baby?"

My ears are not accustomed yet to everybody

speaking English and understanding all the nuances in tones of voice.

But quickly, a more sensitive soul said, "You've got a great kid there. He's a beautiful child."

I had the simultaneous feeling that I was just like these women — I *am* a mother now — but also that I was not just like them. They went across town to one of the New York hospitals to give birth, and several times a day I think of the woman who gave birth to my baby. I feel guilty that I have the beautiful child she gave birth to.

I wanted to cover Kuba's ears and flee, but I tried to stay calm. It was either there or the apartment. And it was only ten fifteen.

By noon I had met several people I think I'll be friends with: Amy, an actress, whose son has delightful rolls of fat; Jane, a journalist, who has a red-headed daughter Celia; and Liz, mother of Luke. Liz had been a businesswoman and freely admitted she had no desire to work outside the home again in her lifetime.

July 4, 1996

When I awoke at five fifty-five to stumble to the shower this morning, before the baby beckoned, I found Willem in the kitchen reading the sports page of the *Times.* "Zydrunas Ilgauskas, a Lithuanian basketball player, has been drafted by the Cleveland Cavaliers," he said.

"Laba Diena." I waved as I headed for the bathroom. I keep turning the word *adopted* over and over in my head. When I watch my sturdy, outgoing sweet boy, I want to know what parts are his genes, how the orphanage affected him, how we've molded him so far. What would he be like if he had never been in an orphanage? What if we had gotten him at birth? I will never know. I will never know. I will never know. I do know that this evening he pulled up in his playpen, which we refer to as his "office," and stood there shaking an empty milk carton for twenty minutes while I made a civilized dinner. When I took him out, I sang "The Star-Spangled Banner," and he did not wince. Before he went to sleep, the three of us watched fireworks over the Hudson from our window and I told him a made-up bedtime story about Paul Revere.

July 8, 1996

This afternoon Sandy, who lives in the building, brought over her daughter, whom she adopted from China. We put the babies in Kuba's "office" and they had a summit conference while we complained about our aching backs, the toil of motherhood, and our children's orphanages, their alma maters. There is an impulse to talk of the time we were in those other lands, and confiding to other women who didn't pack a little suitcase and get flowers in their room after they gave birth feels right. I wonder if, when our children learn to talk (these orphanage children from all over the world, and the ones adopted in this country as well), will there be a special bond?

July 9, 1996

This afternoon, after I trudged in from the playground with Kuba sound asleep, coated with sand in his stroller, I found a gift, two beautiful books at the front door, from an elderly woman in the building, along with a kind note, which ended "You

did what I always wanted to do, but was scared to
... Years ago it wasn't done as much, but I will
always regret my decision."

July 10, 1996

I've been introduced to two terrific young women,
students, one from Poland and another from Brazil,
who will baby-sit when I go back to teaching. I told
Jane at the most recent Mother's Group that I was
worried people would think the baby-sitter from
Poland was Kuba's mother, because there's more of
a resemblance.

"People say things anyway," said Jane. "Last
week my baby-sitter said that while she was pushing Celia on the swing, a woman came up to *her*
and said, 'I've seen your baby-sitter and she does a
great job!' The woman thought I was the baby-
sitter and the baby-sitter was Celia's mother ..."

She made me feel better, but in her case it was
completely clear. She was the mother, the baby-
sitter was the baby-sitter, and there was a confusion. In my case, *I'm* slightly confused. I feel that
I'm Kuba's mother and he is my son, but in the

quiet moments, when I bathe him and wash his belly button, I think of his birth mother. A lovely woman, whose face I've never seen, or perhaps I have, in the face of my lovely son, floats in front of my eyes.

July 11, 1996

Willem took Kuba's papers to the social security office, and next week he should get his social security card in the mail. Within ninety days he is supposed to get his green card, which is really a pink card (which we know, because Willem has one himself). After the card arrives we can fill out more papers for Kuba to become a baby American citizen.

July 18, 1996

A TWA jet, packed with people heading for Paris, crashed over Long Island. Two hundred men, women, and children were killed, including twenty kids from one town of 5,000 in Pennsylvania. We checked on Kuba three times last night. I'm startled at the vastness of the emotion I feel for him. For so long our mission was to become parents, and then to get our baby healthy and safely home. Now that we have him, I'm only beginning to let myself have the normal worries a parent has about keeping him safe and sound.

July 19, 1996

Kuba's social security card arrived promptly in the mail. I believe it is the only facet of this whole adoption process that has gone according to schedule. A treasure chest of gifts also arrived today, by boat from Holland, and after Kuba had fallen asleep, Willem and I shared a pint of chocolate ice cream and opened it. There were over twenty presents, each with a tiny handwritten note from Willem's sisters, aka the Brontës. We carefully unwrapped Willem's cherished childhood toys, the 360-piece puzzle of medieval knights, his favorite book about a little train, *Het Locomotiefje*, and a set of toy soldiers. There was even an embroidered linen bib from his first birthday party forty-five years ago. Life in that parsonage continues to be a marvel to me.

July 21, 1996

Willem and I had an argument last night when he came home from work. He had had a long day at the office, and I've been frustrated by trying to co-ordinate my teaching schedule with the baby-sitters. He brought a small box of raisins for Kuba, and I said he was too young to chew them, and he asked why the book *What to Expect the First Year* talks about babies seeing raisins so much if they aren't allowed to eat them. I said that I wished he would take care of our son for one full day, and we began raising our voices. Kuba stood up in his play-pen and gave us such a bewildered look that we both shut up instantly. I realized it might have been the first argument that ever entered his innocent ears. True, he has now taken a dip in a swimming pool and eaten avocado, but he never had to endure parents arguing over the benefits or perils of raisins.

I felt terrible. I walked over to my desk and

picked up the pinecone that had gotten stuck in the stroller when we left the orphanage and pressed it to my lips. Then I lifted Kuba out of his playpen and went into the bedroom where Willem was lying down. I put Kuba on the bed and the three of us just lay there quietly on our backs for a few minutes.

"Willem," I said hesitantly, "do you think about his birth parents?"

"Only when you ask," he said.

I reached out and held his hand because I needed my hand to be held.

My grandmother once said to me "You think too much," and I have a feeling she would say that now. "Just love your child," she would say.

As the three of us lay on the bed, I understood that much of the grappling in my head was simply part of the daunting dominion of mothers, a place where women often feel misunderstood and men are left baffled, standing alone on the shore.

August 3, 1996

This weekend at my grandmother's ninety-second birthday party was sunny with a gentle breeze. With a child I'm more aware of weather than I've ever been. (Fair skies are a blessing on the day, while pouring rain used to be a romantic delight.) Kuba was welcomed instantly by his cousins from Maine and Colorado and Illinois. My six-year-old nephew said, "I think he's very happy to live here. I don't think he's lonely at all," at which point Kuba crawled over and kissed his foot. Kuba likes to be around people much more than I ever have. A friend from Argentina told me there's a Spanish expression, "All babies are born with bread in their hands," and I think Kuba's bread is bringing a new kind of laughter to our family.

August 27, 1996

Kuba has begun walking at eleven months, and he's like a little giant careening around with a license. Yesterday, just after I was feeling especially proud of him and had sung a fairly rousing rendition of

"Bouncin' Up and Down in My Little Red Wagon," a woman, pushing her daughter on the swings next to me, asked if I was his mother.

"W-well, yes," I stammered. "I'm his mother, but he's adopted." I felt uncomfortable. I didn't know why I was talking to this stranger.

"Oh," she said, "my younger brother was adopted. It's wonderful."

August 28, 1996

Last night in the heat we had the air-conditioners on, with the bedroom doors closed, so we put the baby monitor on. We were so exhausted we went to bed fifteen minutes after Kuba did and were drifting off to the "Rock-a-Bye-Baby" lullaby tape and his little murmurings, when we suddenly heard "And then this guy tells me he doesn't want to get involved, after we'd been sleeping together for a month, and he always brings blueberries!"

I turned to look at Willem, but he'd fallen into a deep sleep, and it took me another few sentences of this conversation to realize the baby monitor was picking up a phone call somewhere in the neighborhood. I could have switched the channel but did not, and as I lay there listening to this woman's tirade about the blueberry cad, my first thought was how could I teach Kuba not to become a cad, and my second thought was how much I looked forward to getting back to teaching, and the call of other people's stories.

Labor Day, 1996

I had turned the kitchen chair around and was sitting on it backward, just like I did in kindergarten when the whole class did the same and we played circus, taking turns doing somersaults in the middle of a circle, when Kuba lilted over to me, put his chubby little hands on my knees, and said "Ma-ma, Ma-ma," for the first time.

I picked him up and cradled him. "Yes, Kuba," I whispered. "I'm your ma-ma."

September 5, 1996

The green card arrived in the mail, and again I called Willem at work and we celebrated as if we'd won the lottery. At lunch I took a picture of Kuba in his high chair, sucking on the coveted card, coated with a bit of applesauce. "This is a prized possession," I told him. "Now some women will want to marry you," but he just dropped the card on the floor.

September 11, 1996

My father is seventy-five today, and Kuba helped blow out the candles on his cake. As I watched the two of them smiling in syncopation, I had the sudden mean memory from a movie I saw years ago, where a little boy was taunted on the playground. "You're adopted! You're adopted!" the other kids screamed. He was adopted. Why was that considered such a horrible thing? How do I tell my son that his mother loved him but could not care for him? When my father was a child, adoptions were

235

kept secret. And I've been showing Kuba photographs of our first meeting in the orphanage.

September 18, 1996

I began teaching this week, and when I was walking to my first class, it took me ten blocks to stop worrying about Kuba's cries when I left. After a few more blocks I'd managed to get the grocery list of zucchini, milk, Pampers, and safety locks for the oven out of my head. Only halfway into the workshop, when I opened my mouth to comment on a student's story about her grandfather who canoed up the Amazon, did I realize I had a large piece of banana on my sleeve. At that moment, my students' names flew out of my head.

September 30, 1996

We're going to fly to Holland for Willem's father's seventy-fourth birthday. He will get to see his grandson and his grandson will get to meet him.

Nobody wants to say it aloud, but this possibly will be a farewell trip. It is difficult to contain the new emotions of parenthood and the prospect of losing a parent at the same time. Kuba was such an angel on the flight from Eastern Europe, but now he wants to walk from dawn until dusk, which does not bode well for this journey.

October 4, 1996

We're in rainy and cold Amsterdam now, and our son's return trip over the Atlantic was not agreeable for him or us or any of our neighboring passengers. We flew on Singapore Airlines, which was efficient and charming as advertised, but Kuba had no interest in sleeping, even though it was an all-night flight. At first the stewardesses clucked over him, but by daybreak their tone was a bit harsh. *"Please, you must sit down. Please,"* they scolded as he strutted down the aisle. I suppose we were lucky he was not reprimanded more harshly, as it's a criminal offense to chew gum in public in Singapore.

October 5, 1996

Yesterday was my father-in-law's birthday. He was dressed and at the door to meet his new grandson, an elegant man, even more so now, with the curious dignity cancer sometimes brings. It was a subdued celebration, with the whole family knowing that this would possibly be his last. At one point he did sit Kuba on his lap and, in a gentle voice, he sang him a Dutch lullaby. Adoption is not as common here and not talked about as much, more like it was thirty years ago in America, and I held Kuba close.

October 8, 1996

We are back in New York. The flight from Amsterdam was not easy, but it was during the day, so at least the other passengers weren't attempting to sleep. We sat next to a couple with a fourteen-month-old girl. The mother was from India and the father was from Singapore. The father said his grandmother lulled babies to sleep by stroking their ears. Willem and I took turns caressing Kuba's ears, but he did not sleep; all he did was giggle.

October 9, 1996

We are still jet-lagged and irritable from the trip, and we just celebrated Kuba's first birthday. He has already attended five birthday parties in his life, but I could not bring myself to orchestrate one. Instead I bought cupcakes and we lit a candle and sang "Happy Birthday" after dinner. All day I felt a shadowed melancholy I could not shake. This day felt like it belonged to his birth mother, and I could not stop wondering what she was feeling. Was she crying? Was she hoping her baby was happy? Was she regretting her choice? One of my students told me her grandson always celebrated his "gottcha" day, the day his parents first got him. Perhaps we'll celebrate the day in June when we officially became a family.

"Next year," I whispered in Kuba's ear, while he squashed a cupcake in his little fist. "Next year I promise we'll have a great party."

My son is now one year old, but I've only been a mother for five months. I'm not sure what that particular equation means, except there is something surreal about it. I wonder when I'll feel like I've caught up to him.

November 1, 1996

Last night was Halloween; we dressed Kuba as a cowboy, and he waddled around to our neighbors, throwing his hat down at every door. When people cooed over how cute he was, I said "Thank you" for the first time, instead of "He is, isn't he?"

November 2, 1996

I celebrated my forty-third birthday, and in honor of that occasion I took Kuba to get a new pair of shoes. When the salesman had tied snappy blue-green oxfords on his sturdy feet, he said, "Now walk to Grandma." I assumed he was talking about someone else, until I realized there was nobody else in the store. I was able to laugh, but only when the salesman freely admitted that he was only a year older than I and had five grandchildren of his own.

November 3, 1996

Today, as I juggled with the stroller and groceries and Kuba, I opened the mailbox to find a thick envelope. I ripped it open as soon as I managed to wedge myself in the front door. Out spilled all the papers we had filed for U.S. citizenship. A brief letter insisted that we had sent the papers to the wrong place. I called our lawyer, and after several more calls it was ascertained that in fact we had sent them to the correct place but now needed one additional form to fill out. We had sent a check for ten dollars too much! I addressed a new envelope, wrote a new check, and sent the package off to the original address. Now we must wait three more months before we will be notified of the swearing-in ceremony.

I feel like I have a hummingbird beating in my chest, a fast fluttering that makes it difficult to sleep. I want all this paperwork done. I have no shelves left in my brain for such matters.

Thanksgiving, 1996

My brother visited, bearing several plastic vehicles for his new nephew, who immediately fell to his knees and began making appropriate car sounds. Sweet potatoes and pumpkin pie touched Kuba's lips for the first time, and he was delighted, even if he doesn't have his American legal papers. After dinner he marched around shaking everybody's hand and I thought that if he's doing so well, we should all be abandoned at birth, and I also thought his birth mother would be very proud of him.

November 29, 1996

Last week we received a book as a gift called *The Day We Met You* by Phoebe Koehler, and Kuba is enchanted. At least three times a day he drags it off the shelf, climbs up on the couch, holds it out to me, and demands, "More." I read it to him over and over, and each time he bends over and kisses key pages, the page with the dog, the page with the teddy bear, and the page at the end with the mother and father and the new baby. My friend Laura says

I'm beginning to sound evangelical when I tell her I feel privileged to watch him put together his world each day.

December 16, 1996

I'm getting sick. My joints ache and my throat is sore. Finishing the semester, seeing distant friends who pass through New York on their vacations, holiday shopping . . . I would like one day to sleep late, just one tiny day. But then I see it is twenty below zero in Eastern Europe, and I think of the orphanage and I wonder if we should go back for another child.

December 30, 1996

It is almost the new year and I have the flu. Mothers are not supposed to be sick. I feel terrible and terrible that I feel terrible. I know Kuba is having a grand time with Willem. Willem has been with him from 7 A.M. this morning until he put him to bed at night. He took him to the playground for

243

several hours, and then to the Museum of Natural History to climb endless steps and gaze at his favorite stuffed polar bear. Willem fed Kuba three meals, two snacks, changed five diapers, bathed him, read to him, sang him lullabies, and settled him into a serene sleep, a full twelve-hour shift.

"You didn't think I could do it," he said as he sat on the bed and I dozed in 103 degree temperature, ornamented with diaper cream on my sore nose.

"I never said that," I murmured, but even in my altered state, I knew I was happy.

January 7, 1997

I'm over the flu and am getting my strength back but don't have anywhere near the resilient energy Willem and Kuba have. Willem has begun training for the New York marathon next November. Last night he came home from work and went out into the winter dark to run. When he returned, dripping with sweat and snow in his hair, Kuba ran to the door with a soccer ball, yelling "Out! Out!" I have a strong sense that home is just a way-station for both these boys. My husband and son like to be out, out.

January 20, 1997

Yesterday Liz, who is more serene than most women I've met to be "just a mother," and I wheeled our boys in their strollers by the Hudson River as a strong wind blew. We talked and talked about our husbands and sons, as our icy breaths blew up into the winter sky. As we passed houseboats bouncing on the rough water and buoy bells ringing, our boys held each other's hands. I'm at ease with Liz because she never asks questions I don't want to answer. Our sons are our sons and we take it from there.

February 1, 1997

We have received three identical gifts of "baby books," journals to record every smile, step, and sound of our son, but in each one there are pages with daunting headings such as "The Day of Your

Birth" and "What People Brought You in the Hospital." And each book begins with an innocent enough family tree complete with daintily painted green leaves, but each one gives me a small headache. I often show Kuba photographs of his new family as well as pictures in a scrapbook I've made of Lithuania, but when I see a page marked "Great-Great-Grandparents," I get an image of my ancestors from Eastern Europe and his birth ancestors from Eastern Europe and there are too many people in the frame.

February 8, 1997

Willem and Kuba have become quite a team. They go off on outings on the weekends, with Kuba in the backpack, and they return like victorious soldiers from foreign lands. Each time Willem introduces Kuba to new delicacies—hot dogs with sauerkraut, Vietnamese summer rolls, piña colada to drink . . . and I'm in awe. When I see the delight in Kuba's eyes, I can see him as a young man, perhaps with a friend, back in town for a night or two, en route to more adventures. I think, although I have no proof, that if I had given birth to him, I would feel more possessive of him. I have a strong sense that his time with us is some kind of a gift, although I'm aware that Laura would say I'm sounding evangelical again.

February 11, 1997

Today, as Kuba ran around the lobby of our building with my apartment keys and I had my arms full of trucks and one foot on the stroller to keep it from tipping over, I unlocked the mailbox to find an official-looking letter from the Immigration Department. I ripped it open with appropriately trembling hands.

PLEASE APPEAR AT THE DEPARTMENT OF HEALTH
125 WORTH STREET
FOR NATURALIZATION CEREMONIES
March 21, 1997 11:00 A.M.
Proper attire required

I dropped the trucks, let the stroller crash to the ground, ran to Kuba, picked him up, and swung him around. "Hello, Mr. America," I whispered, at which point he squirmed away from me and continued with his tasks.

February 12, 1997

Read student work
Pampers
Fire truck
Birthday presents for twin two-year-olds
Get proper attire for Kuba for citizenship ceremony

February 23, 1997

We had our first sleepaway, just the grown-ups, twenty-one hours of freedom. Kuba stayed home with one of his adored baby-sitters. For the first three hours all we could do was trade imitations of him saying his latest two words, the all-important "truck" and "bus," as well as various animal sounds in Dutch and English that he particularly enjoys (cows, owls, and dogs), but finally we were able to settle into more adult forms of entertainment and recalled why we had married each other. Although we woke up the next morning precisely at 6 A.M., the fact that we could have slept later if we had wanted to gave us great joy.

March 6, 1997

This morning on the playground Kuba played with a little girl adopted from China and a little boy adopted from Ecuador. I don't know if the kids have some extrasensory perception about other adopted children, but the adoptive parents scope each other out. We're like magnets for one another. And we all begin to tell our stories, usually out-of-earshot of the children. We answer one another's questions that would feel intrusive if asked by anyone else.

March 8, 1997

Today, as I sat on the floor in Kuba's room, he gathered all his cars, trucks, and trains, one by one, and meticulously stacked them in my lap. After he had succeeded in balancing this awkward pile, he insisted on sitting on it. He sat that way, in this vehicular nest, for longer than he had ever sat on my lap before.

March 16, 1997

At 4 A.M. I woke up with the recollection that we had received a baby present, a formal blue-and-white shirt with suspenders and quite snazzy pants. At six fifteen I wrestled Kuba into this outfit and it all actually fit. I quickly, mercifully, let him return to running around in just his diaper but was relieved to have found the proper attire for his citizenship ceremony. Of course Kuba has no interest in my fussy preparations, but this last leg of the paper highway apparently means a lot to me.

March 23, 1997

Our son is now an American citizen.

Neither Willem or I slept the night before the event, frightened we would oversleep, which is not humanly possible anymore. We awoke to a strangely humid morning, with Kuba bursting with energy. He marched around in his suspenders and trousers, bare-chested, looking very proud of himself. When we were able to coax him into the shirt, Willem took out a tiny blue bow tie he had found, but Kuba would have none of it. Each time Willem tried to clip it on, he pulled it off and hurled it across the room. I ended up wearing it in my hair. I wore the same outfit I wore in court in Vilnius, and Willem wore a suit and the bow tie he had worn at our wedding.

The ceremony was far downtown, but we arrived at the government buildings a half-hour early. The Department of Health is an old building, not unlike the KGB building in Lithuania, with heavy walls and steps bearing witness to generations of daily struggles with bureaucracy. Kuba insisted on climbing each step his own way, which involved going up two then going down one, before continuing the ascent, and he considered holding hands with us far too babyish. The second-floor meeting room was dark and stuffy, with rows of metal seats facing a stage that was bare except for a podium and an American flag.

We handed our invitations to the clerk, then signed two forms saying we were who we said we were, parents of our son. We were then given a round sticker that said "Go for It," with a small decal of an American flag. I stuck it on Kuba's back. We were also given a large envelope containing his Certificate of Naturalization and a personal letter from Bill and Hillary Clinton.

Within fifteen minutes the room echoed with chattering children from all over the world, many of them dressed in red-white-and-blue ensembles, and their slightly harried parents who had managed to dress themselves decently but not with as much style. We soon learned there were thirty children from eleven countries, ranging in age from ten months to fourteen years. Most of the adults had some kind of camera hanging around their necks. I had the strong sense that I was at a reunion when, in fact, I had never seen any of these people before. The woman next to us, holding a little girl from Bolivia, said, "They call every child up individually and shake hands. At least that's what they did with my older children."

❀   ❀   ❀

Eleven o'clock came and went, and then eleven fifteen, and now the atmosphere was like an overcrowded children's birthday party at which neither the magician or the cake has arrived. Everybody was tired and hungry, and those wise enough to bring bags of fruit and pretzels shared them with everybody else. Some children had fallen asleep in their parents' arms, while others appeared to be sailing around the room. Kuba thought it a great game to climb the steps to the stage, walk across it grinning, tug on the American flag, then climb down the other side, over and over again.

Finally we were told that because two families were late, the ceremony would not take place for fifteen more minutes.

At eleven thirty a scratchy tape recording of "The Star-Spangled Banner" began to play and Willem caught our son in one of his transstage journeys and carried him to our seats.

A female judge approached the lectern and thanked us for coming and said that this was her favorite part of her job. She then apologized for the delay. Because we were starting so late, the children would not go to the stage individually. She asked us all to stand for the Oath of Allegiance, not the Pledge of Allegiance (That came next), but the oath for new citizens, a mass swearing-in. All the grown-ups stood and held their children in various states, some asleep, some wriggling around. Kuba sat beaming on Willem's shoulders. The grown-ups were told to raise their right hands, and some people held up their children's hands as well.

I hereby declare, on oath, that I absolutely and entirely renounce and abjure all allegiance and fidelity to any foreign prince, potentate, state of sovereignty of whom or which I have heretofore been a subject or citizen; that I will support and defend the Constitution, and laws, of the United States of America against all enemies, foreign and domestic; that I will bear true faith and allegiance to the same; that I will bear arms on behalf of the United States when required by the law; that I will perform noncombatant service in the armed forces of the United States when required by the law; that I will perform work of national importance, under civilian direction, when required by the law; and that I take this obligation freely, without any mental reservation, or purpose of evasion; so help me God.

There were many teary eyes in the house at this point, mine included. I cried tears of relief, realizing we had come so far and we finally had a child nobody could take away, but I was also weeping at the notion of Kuba forswearing allegiance and fidelity to the place of his birth, which seemed harsh and abrupt, especially when he had no say in the matter. And I cried at the thought of my baby ever having to go off to war.

After the ceremony there was a burst of applause and much kissing and hugging. I was sure the walls of the room could feel our collective exhaustion, of the long journeys of all the parents and all our children.

April 2, 1997

Willem and I have begun dating each other once a week. We usually can't make ourselves stay up past ten P.M., and it has been more than once that we have walked slowly around the block several times to fill up our allotted time. But last night we had a craving for Eastern European food and found ourselves at a little shop called Rush'n'Express, wolfing down blinis and blintzes.

April 8, 1997

Today we took Kuba to be photographed for his U.S. passport. When he sat on Willem's lap, the photographer said, "The apple doesn't fall far from the tree. Your son looks exactly like you."

Willem and I just nodded.

April 18, 1997

This afternoon, when Kuba awoke from his nap on the wrong side of his crib, I two-stepped around his room to bring a smile to his face. As he began to giggle, I could see my grandfather, with top hat and cane, doing a soft-shoe shuffle in the 1950s for his six grandchildren on a rainy spring afternoon. I wish he had met his new great-grandson.

April 24, 1997

One of my students invited us to sheep-shearing festivities at her farm in Connecticut. Kuba has become our calling card for an array of new activities. We drove north for over two hours on a windy Saturday morning. When we arrived, Kuba burst out of the car and ran after the sheep through the mud and last patches of snow, throwing his arms around the animals when they let him. Later he was entranced when he saw their great soft coats being shaved from their backs and the piles of wool that were loaded into trucks.

In the afternoon, after a feast in the barn of herb soup, robust sandwiches, cakes and cookies, our host told us that some of the baby lambs who could not be nursed would be bottle-fed. Kuba ran to this event with great glee, and when he held a bottle to a lamb's guzzling lips, he was a natural, caring for a child whose mother could not do so herself.

April 28, 1997

I have sand in my shoes all the time now from the sandbox. When I teach I feel sand between my toes, but I'm no longer startled by it. Sand is all over the house, no matter how much I try to shake things out before we go inside. I'm like the woman in the Japanese film *Woman in the Dunes*, endlessly trying to sweep up, but for some reason I'm secretly delighted by it. I never believed I'd ever have so many vehicles or so much sand scattered around my home.

May 1, 1997

Today is our sixth anniversary. I do believe that making love to your husband while your son is calling "Ma-ma-Ma-ma" from his crib down the hall is an extraordinary sensation.

May 11, 1997 Mother's Day

We spent my first Mother's Day at my aunt and uncle's house in the country. There were four generations, great-grandmother, grandmother, mother, and son. We ate outside at a table on the soft grass, the same place where I had played as a toddler and made up intricate games about make-believe babies, pulling them endlessly around in my red wagon. After lunch, as my husband and son kicked a ball back and forth in the dappled light, I could see no seam in our stitched-together family.

At one point Kuba darted over to me, pointed up to the sky, and said an entire sentence in almost-decipherable child babble. In that instant, I realized that soon this story of adoption will no longer be mine, but his story, to confide to others about in his words and to keep to himself when he chooses.

May 14, 1997

A Dutch friend called at six this morning American time. I had just lifted Kuba from his crib. I breathed in his sweet, sleepy smell as I heard her talk faintly across the Atlantic Ocean. The connection was not good, as if there were fish chewing on the wire, but I could hear what she said.

"I'm going to get a baby," she said over and over. "I'm going to get a child."

I knew she meant "have" a baby, but I saw no need to correct her, no need in the world.

To my dear parents, grandmother and whole family, who waited and welcomed by my side

To M., who is part angel and part ambassador

To the writer-mothers, Laurel Davis, Sheila Kohler, Carol Magun, Conan Putnam, Nahid Rachlin, Melissa Shiflett, Abby Thomas, and Carol Weston, who taught me it was possible to be both

To Lisa Ross, my sage agent, who patiently helped navigate in my first attempt at a book about "real life"

To Jennifer Barth, my editor, whose keen eye and perfect-pitch ear shaped this story

To Charles Salzberg, who connected the dots

To Marc Rabinowitz, who first encouraged me to take my pages out of a shopping bag

To Doris and Mark Berger, Marcy and Mark Bishop, Michael Collins, Thelma Connor, Whitney and Peter Hansen, Eileen Heaney, Judith Hirsch, Corrie Horshinski, Myrna Jacobs, Anna Monardo, Bari Moss, Silvia Olarte, Mary Rae, Jane Rosenman, Andy Schlesinger, Barbara Schultz, and David Slavin who have been there before, during and after

To the Writer's Voice and Sarah Lawrence, who permitted the most flexible maternity leave on earth

To my students, whose remarkable stories taught me to practice what I preach

To all the shining people, in this country and Eastern Europe, who helped us on our journey

To Rosane and Hanna, who help care for K. with such stamina and good spirits

To my child, who is teaching me everything else

And to everybody waiting for the baby boat